$f$**P**

# Arguing the World

## The New York Intellectuals in Their Own Words

## Joseph Dorman

**The Free Press**

New York  London  Toronto  Singapore  Sydney

**THE FREE PRESS**

A Division of Simon & Schuster Inc.
1230 Avenue of the Americas
New York, NY 10020

Copyright © 2000 by Joseph Dorman.

The Free Press and colophon are trademarks of
Simon & Schuster, Inc.

Designed by Kim Llewellyn

Manufactured in the United States of America

10 9 8 7 6 5 4 3 2 1

Library of Congress Cataloging-in-Publication Data

    Arguing the world : the New York intellectuals in their own words /
[edited by] Joseph Dorman.
       p.  cm.
    Includes bibliographical references (p.  ) and index.
    1. Intellectuals—New York (State)—New York—History—20th century.
2. Intellectuals—New York (State)—New York—Interviews.  3. New York
(N.Y.)—Intellectual life—20th century.  4. United States—Intellectual life—
20th century.  I. Dorman, Joseph, 1958–  .
    F128.52.A75  2000     00-041076
    974.7'1043—dc21

ISBN 0-684-86279-4

*October 23, 2000*

To my mother, Eleanor Dorman,
and to the memory of my father,
Jack Dorman (1915–99)

# Contents

# Acknowledgments

Armed with the biographer's license to ask almost anything, I've had the great fortune to have spent numerous hours talking with Irving Kristol, Nathan Glazer, and Daniel Bell, and I wish to thank them for their enormous generosity in agreeing to participate in both the documentary and this book. While I fear they may have had no idea exactly what they were getting themselves into, they nevertheless amiably persevered, particularly through the many inconveniences of the filmmaking process. And though his untimely death prevented me from spending as much time with Irving Howe, he, too, proved generous at a moment when he had already begun to suffer from the illness which would eventually take his life.

In his autobiography, *A Margin of Hope*, Howe tells the story of *Partisan Review* editor Philip Rahv calling fellow New York intellectual and art critic Meyer Schapiro "to check some fact and then listening openmouthed for an hour to a lecture providing answer, background and foreground, until Rahv turned to his wife and said, 'I've just received an MA over the telephone!'" Being in the presence of these four men has also seemed to me a graduate education unlike any other I might more conventionally have received.

Thanks and acknowledgments are also due to my friend and colleague Jonathan Oppenheim, a wonderful film editor and arguing companion who was instrumental in originally helping to shape this material. During the making of the film I also relied on the insights of Morris Dickstein, Arnold Labaton, Gail Segal, and Emily Shapiro. Terry Cooney's research led me to the excerpts from James Farrell's diaries as well as the correspondence between

Leon Trotsky and Dwight Macdonald quoted in chapter 4. As well, I am indebted to John Patrick Diggins, Deborah Dash Moore, Russell Jacoby, Neil Jumonville, Maurice Isserman, William O'Neill, and Ronald Radosh.

My longtime friend Alex Goulder proved a supportive and wise reader of the present manuscript. His sharp insights, suggestions and sense of humor have made the book better than it otherwise might have been.

The documentary film on which this book is based was funded largely by the National Endowment for the Humanities. In a time when it seems harder and harder to make serious films, they remain a critical source of funding. Without them, *Arguing the World* could not have been made. I would also like to acknowledge the support of Tamara Robinson and WNET in New York, Richard Gilder, the New York Council for the Humanities, and the National Foundation for Jewish Culture. At The Free Press, I wish to thank my editor, Paul Golob, whose expertise and thoughtful suggestions helped transform the original film into this book. His assistant, Alys Yablon, helped guide me through the intricacies of readying a manuscript for press. And finally, thanks are due to publisher Paula Barker Duffy, who first approached me with the idea of the film translating to the printed page and therefore without whom this book would not exist.

# The Participants

**Daniel Bell** (b. 1919) is the Henry Ford II Professor of Social Sciences, Emeritus, at Harvard University and previously taught at the University of Chicago and at Columbia University. He has held senior editorial positions at *The New Leader* and at *Fortune* and is the author of *The End of Ideology*, *The Coming of Post-Industrial Society*, and *The Cultural Contradictions of Capitalism*, among other works. With Irving Kristol he cofounded *The Public Interest*, and most recently he cofounded *Correspondence*, a quarterly journal of ideas and cultural commentary.

**Nathan Glazer** (b. 1923) is Professor of Education and Sociology, Emeritus, at Harvard University and has also taught at the University of California at Berkeley. He is the author or coauthor of numerous works of sociology, including *The Lonely Crowd* (with David Riesman), *Beyond the Melting Pot* (with Daniel Patrick Moynihan), *The Limits of Social Policy*, and *We Are All Multiculturalists Now*. A former assistant at *Commentary* magazine, he is presently coeditor of *The Public Interest* magazine.

**Irving Howe** (1920–93) was Distinguished Professor of English at the City University of New York as well as the founder and editor of *Dissent* magazine. A longtime leader of America's socialist movement, he was also an influential literary critic and scholar of Jewish history. His many books include *Politics and the Novel*, *World of Our Fathers*, *Socialism and America*, and *The American Newness*.

**Irving Kristol** (b. 1920) is the John M. Olin Distinguished Fellow at the American Enterprise Institute for Public Policy Research in Washington, D.C. Previously he was an assistant editor at *Commen-*

*tary* magazine, and coeditor of the magazine *Encounter*, before becoming an editor at Basic Books. In 1965, he and Daniel Bell cofounded *The Public Interest*, for which he has served as coeditor ever since. He is the author of several books, including *On the Democratic Idea in America*, *Reflections of a Neoconservative,* and *Neo-Conservatism: The Autobiography of an Idea.*

**Lionel Abel** (b. 1910) is a playwright and literary critic who has contributed to *The New Republic* and *Dissent* among other publications; he was an early member of the *Partisan Review* circle and is the author of *The Intellectual Follies: A Memoir of the Literary Venture in New York and Paris.*

**Saul Bellow** (b. 1915) published his first series in *Partisan Review*. He is the author of more than thirteen novels, including *The Adventures of Augie March*, *Henderson the Rain King*, *Herzog*, *Humboldt's Gift,* and *Ravelstein*. He received the Nobel Prize for Literature in 1976.

**Paul Berman** (b. 1949) is a literary and political journalist. As an undergraduate at Columbia University in the 1960s, he was a member of Students for a Democratic Society, and he is most recently the author of *A Tale of Two Utopias: The Political Journey of the Generation of 1968.*

**William F. Buckley, Jr.** (b. 1925) is the founder and publisher of *National Review* and a longtime leader of the modern conservative political movement. He is the author of numerous books on politics, language, and culture, as well as a series of espionage novels. From 1966 to 1999 he was the creator and host of the PBS public-affairs show *Firing Line.*

**Helen Frankenthaler** (b. 1928) is a leading member of the second generation of Abstract Expressionist painters and a pioneer of "Color-Field" painting. A recipient of numerous awards, her work was the subject of a retrospective by the Musuem of Modern Art in 1989.

**Todd Gitlin** (b. 1943) is a professor of sociology at New York University and a former president and founding member of Students for a Democratic Society. He is the author of a number of books, including *The Sixties: Years of Hope, Days of Rage*, and *The Twilight of Common Dreams: Why America Is Wracked by Culture Wars*.

**Jackie Goldberg** (b. 1945) is a Democratic member of the Los Angeles City Council and a former leader of the Free Speech Movement at the University of California at Berkeley.

**Tom Hayden** (b. 1939) is a Democratic state senator in California and a former president of Students for a Democratic Society. As an undergraduate student at the University of Michigan in 1962, he helped to draft the "Port Huron Statement," the founding document of the New Left.

**Tom Hurwitz** (b. 1947) is a director of photography for documentary films and was a member of Students for a Democratic Society as an undergraduate at Columbia University.

**Alfred Kazin** (1915–99) was a distinguished literary critic and a graduate of the City College of New York. He is the author of numerous books, among them *On Native Grounds*, *The American Procession*, and *A Walker in the City*.

**Seymour Martin Lipset** (b. 1922) is a professor of sociology at George Mason University and a graduate of the City College of New York. He is the author of *Political Man*, *The First New Nation*, and *American Exceptionalism*, among many other books.

**Victor Navasky** (b. 1932) is the longtime editor of *The Nation* and is presently its publisher. He is the author of *Naming Names*, an exploration of the McCarthy years, and other books.

**William Phillips** (b.1907), a literary critic, founded *Partisan Review* in 1934 along with Philip Rahv and is still its editor today. He is the author of *A Partisan View*.

**Norman Podhoretz** (b. 1930) was the editor of *Commentary* for thirty-five years and is currently editor-at-large for the magazine. He is the author of *Making It, Breaking Ranks*, and *Ex-Friends*.

**Phillip Selznick** (b. 1919) is Professor Emeritus of Law and Sociology at the University of California at Berkeley. He is a graduate of the City College of New York and is the author, most recently, of *The Moral Commonwealth: Social Theory and the Promise of Community*.

**Diana Trilling** (1905-96) was a literary critic and author of, among other books, *Mrs. Harris: The Death of the Scarsdale Diet Doctor* and *The Beginning of the Journey: The Marriage of Diana and Lionel Trilling*.

**Michael Walzer** (b. 1935) is a political philosopher at the Institute for Advanced Study in Princeton and coeditor of *Dissent* magazine. He is the author of *Just and Unjust Wars, Spheres of Justice*, and, most recently, *On Toleration*, among other works.

**Jack Weinberg** (b. 1940) is an environmental activist. He was a leading member of the Berkeley Free Speech Movement.

**James Q. Wilson** (b. 1931) is a professor of Strategy and Organization at the Anderson School of Business at UCLA and is a specialist in criminology. His many books include *The Moral Sense and American Government*. He is a longtime contributor to *The Public Interest*.

# The New York Jewish Intellectuals

## The Elders
COMING OF AGE IN THE LATE 1920S AND EARLY 1930S

Elliot Cohen
Sidney Hook
Philip Rahv
Lionel Trilling
Meyer Schapiro
William Phillips
Hannah Arendt★
Diana Trilling

GENTILE COUSINS
Max Eastman
Edmund Wilson
Reinhold Niebuhr
Fred Dupee
Dwight Macdonald
James T. Farrell

MAGAZINES
*Menorah Journal*
*Partisan Review*

## The Younger Brothers
COMING OF AGE IN THE MID AND LATE 1930S

Alfred Kazin
Richard Hofstadter
Saul Bellow★★
Delmore Schwartz
Bernard Malamud
Harold Rosenberg
Clement Greenberg
Lionel Abel
Paul Goodman
Isaac Rosenfeld

EUROPEAN RELATIVES
Nicola Chiaramonte
George Lichtheim

GENTILE COUSINS
Mary McCarthy
Elizabeth Hardwick
James Baldwin
Arthur Schlesinger, Jr.
William Barrett
Richard Chase
Ralph Ellison

MAGAZINES
*Commentary*
*The Nation*
*The New Republic*
*Partisan Review*
*Politics*

## The Second Generation
COMING OF AGE IN THE LATE 1930S AND EARLY 1940S

Daniel Bell
Irving Howe
Leslie Fiedler★★
Robert Warshow
Gertrude Himmelfarb
Irving Kristol
Melvin Lasky
Nathan Glazer
S. M. Lipset★★
David Bazelon

GENTILE COUSINS
Murray Kempton
C. Wright Mills

MAGAZINES
*Commentary*
*Dissent*
*Encounter*★★
*The New Leader*
*The Public Interest*

## The Younger Brothers
COMING OF AGE IN THE LATE 1940S AND EARLY 1950S

Norman Podhoretz
Steven Marcus
Robert Brustein
Midge Decter
Jason Epstein
Robert Silvers
Susan Sontag
Theodore Solotaroff
Norman Mailer
Philip Roth

GENTILE COUSINS
Michael Harrington
"The Paris Review"†

MAGAZINES
*Commentary*
*New York Review of Books*
*Partisan Review*

---

★Arrived later, yet became one of the elders.
★★Outside New York but had status as members.
†The social and intellectual coterie that included George Plimpton and William Styron.

Adapted from "The 'Intelligentsia' in American Society" in *The Winding Passage* by Daniel Bell. *Courtesy of Daniel Bell.*

# A Note on the Text

The following is a much-expanded oral history of the careers and evolving political beliefs of Daniel Bell, Nathan Glazer, Irving Howe, and Irving Kristol, based on my documentary film *Arguing the World*. I have been grateful for the opportunity to include in this book much material that had to be omitted from the original film. I have also taken the opportunity to conduct new interviews with my main subjects and to add new voices where appropriate.

Among the key voices in the text are those of other New York intellectuals who were still alive—and willing to be interviewed—during the time I was working on the film and the book. Their views play a crucial role, I believe, in helping the reader to understand the intellectual milieu within which the four men thought and acted. But I do not wish to give the impression that this is a comprehensive oral history of the New York intellectual group. By the time I began my research, many New York intellectuals had already passed away, and others died during the course of the production, making such a task, even had I wanted to undertake it, an impossible one.

# 1. A Lifetime in Argument

THE NEW YORK WRITERS . . . CAN SPEAK BITTERLY ABOUT EACH
OTHER'S WORK AND OPINIONS, THEY MAY NOT SEE EACH OTHER FROM
YEAR'S START TO YEAR'S END, BUT THEY ARE NERVOUSLY ALERT TO
ONE ANOTHER'S JUDGMENTS. ATTENTION IS PAID—WHETHER FROM
WARRANTED RESPECT OR COLLECTIVE VANITY OR PROVINCIAL NARROW-
NESS IT HARDLY MATTERS.

—*Irving Howe,* The New York Intellectuals,
A Chronicle and A Critique

NATHAN GLAZER FIRST SET EYES on *Partisan Review* in the early
forties when a fellow radical at the City College of New York
thrust a copy of the magazine into his hands, insisting, in the way
only one neophyte can to another, "You have to read this. It's very
important." In high school, I can remember a teacher placing *The
New York Review of Books* in my hands with the same insistence of
tone, that italicized gravity that Glazer had heard, and understanding something akin to what Glazer had seen some forty
years earlier: that the pages set before me were a gateway to
another, higher world—one Daniel Bell would describe as "a
world of imagination, a world of ideas."

For Glazer, along with his friends Irving Kristol, Daniel Bell,
and Irving Howe, that world first revealed itself at City College, a
school that opened its arms to New York City's aspiring poor.
During the Depression years when the four attended City College, it was heavily Jewish, a boys' college filled with the sons of
New York's immigrant Jewish population from the Bronx, Brooklyn, and the Lower East Side. Columbia University, the city's pre-

eminent college, considered itself a training ground for the city's Protestant elite. Its secret quota for Jewish students, along with a lack of jobs during the Depression, swelled the ranks of applicants to City College and turned the school into a remarkable factory for Jewish talent. Its 1937 class remains the only one in American history to graduate three future Nobel laureates.

In those years the college was gripped by radical fervor. While the truly political students were a minority on campus (most of its students working and hoping against Depression-era odds to find future careers in professions such as teaching or engineering), they were a vocal and ardent minority. But at the right moment, these committed radicals could spark a campus-wide conflagration. Just a few years before the four young men arrived, a visiting delegation of students from Mussolini's fascist Italy became the occasion for a near-riot in a college assembly, leading to the suspension and expulsion of large numbers of students and countless days of student strikes. A twin-headed effigy—one half college president Frederick Robinson, the other Il Duce himself—was ceremoniously set aflame by the angry protesters.

By the time Bell, Kristol, Howe, and Glazer arrived, the campus had become home to a feverish student radicalism that burned with the concentrated energy of a hard, glowing ember. The defining issue for these young radicals had become the nature of radicalism itself, a question posed by Soviet Russia, the world's first socialist state. Was Soviet leader Joseph Stalin the true prophet of Marxism or had he corrupted the ideals and principles of the Soviet revolution? In the college's cafeteria alcoves, radicals gathered in constant, uninterrupted discussion from morning to night—the anti-Stalinist opponents of the Soviet Union in alcove one, their Stalinist foes in alcove two. Of course, as City College alumnus Philip Selznick recalled, "in those days having a discussion meant arguing about something and doing it at the top of your lungs!" Highly competitive, intellectually agile, and loudly vocal, the young radicals were attempting to grasp the nature of their crumbling world through the lens of Marxism; Bell, Kristol, Howe, and Glazer all found an ideological home among the anti-Stalinist contingent. "College students are very good at talk," sixties radical Todd Gitlin remembered of his own famously talkative generation. Yet while this later generation of radicals would speak of striving for a consensus among peers, the young radicals of the thirties were interested only in doing intellectual battle. Did they know then that their argument would last a lifetime?

For early radical converts like Bell and Howe, the argument had begun even earlier, on the streets of their immigrant neighborhoods. As young street corner speakers, they had harangued and argued with impromptu crowds over the fate of the American economy and the blessings of socialism. But the nature of the argument deepened and changed at City College. Over the course of those years, Marxist thought would provide a kind of mental chrysalis, allowing each young man to transform himself, almost unconsciously, from would-be radical to nascent intellectual. They had thought that argument would help to confirm the correct path toward political salvation, but in practice, their interest in politics proved a bridge toward a life of intellectual inquiry. *Partisan Review* and its coterie of writers would inspire them to make the crossing.

In the 1930s, *Partisan Review*—the magazine that had been placed in Glazer's hands—was a journal that had to be read if one was to consider oneself a knowledgeable member of the anti-Stalinist left. Though it would go on to exercise great cultural influence after the Second World War, at the time *PR* was still an obscure publication with a circulation perhaps in the hundreds. What mattered in the end was that *PR* had tapped into the cultural and political avant-garde, publishing major figures like T. S. Eliot, Edmund Wilson, and even the great exiled Soviet leader Leon Trotsky himself.

The magazine and its editors were an anomaly in the late thirties and early forties. Like their City College counterparts, they were a minority within a minority. Even in Greenwich Village where the magazine was headquartered, home to bohemians and artists in flight from bourgeois America, *Partisan Review*'s anti-Stalinism represented a distinctly unpopular point of view. Most writers and intellectuals had become members of the Communist party or "fellow travelers," whereas *Partisan Review* was edited by two Communist renegades, Philip Rahv and William Phillips. For its writers and readers alike, the small size of the magazine's following became a badge of honor; its pages revealed to initiates the esoterica of modernism and Marxism, the era's new secular religions. It was probably no accident, as Irving Howe pointed out, that Philip Rahv's surname, chosen as a radical alias, meant "rabbi" in Hebrew.

When I first plunged seriously into *The New York Review of Books* in college, I had no notion that it was a kind of grandson to *PR*, one of the last in a line of journals founded by a group of thinkers known as the "New York intellectuals." Nor was I aware that its anti-Communist worldview could be traced back to the minority-within-a-minority that had once huddled around *Partisan Review*. But I found myself drawn to its steady stream of articles by Eastern European dissidents and émigrés, and admiring these latter-day intellectual opponents of Communism whose lives and work bent against its political totalitarianism and against the moral corruption of the societies it had created.

Many years later, when I stumbled upon an essay by Irving Kristol about his experiences at City College with a group of young radicals (including Bell, Glazer, and Howe), I was struck by the experiences of these "premature" anti-Communists. A few years after that, the essay led me to begin the documentary film *Arguing the World*, and, subsequently, to write this book.

My interest in this group's early anti-Stalinism was heightened by my admiration for their later accomplishments. They were all influential intellectuals whose work I had read without ever being aware of their common origins or of their lifelong relationships with one another. And then there was the fact of their disparate political trajectories. They had begun their lives together as young radicals, and yet Kristol had ended up a confirmed neoconservative; Howe, a committed socialist; Glazer, a political pragmatist chary of both liberal and conservative verities; and Bell, in his own words, a liberal in politics, a socialist in economics, and a conservative in culture.

Of whatever ideological disposition, they were all men of ideas. In addition to founding and editing the socialist magazine *Dissent*, Howe, who did much to revive interest in Yiddish literature and culture, was a noted literary critic and author of *Politics and the Novel* (1957). Bell, a longtime sociologist and social theorist, was responsible for one of the earliest and farthest-reaching theories of contemporary social change in *The Coming of Post-Industrial Society* (1973). Glazer, a sociologist, did seminal work in ethnicity in *Beyond the Melting Pot* (1964), in addition to his work on urbanism, architecture, and social policy. Kristol, less an academic than his friends, has spent a life as an influential editor and essayist, becoming in his later years an adept at the politics of ideas, reinvigorating modern conservatism through his writings on culture and public policy.

I set out to understand what had led these four men to take such different political paths as their lives traversed some of the most extraordinary events in postwar America. As young writers in the fifties they were embroiled in the controversies swirling around Joseph McCarthy; they clashed with the New Left as middle-aged professors in the sixties; and they were, in part, responsible, as members of what became known as the neoconservative movement, for the reevaluation of liberal public policy that occurred in the eighties and nineties. *Arguing the World* is thus a group portrait of the political and intellectual growth of these four men over the course of sixty years.

From reading Kristol's essay grew years of research and interviews. The world of the New York intellectuals was vanishing as I approached it, the group at the time in their seventies and eighties.

Some, like Philip Rahv, had died years before; others, like Dwight Macdonald, more recently; still others, like Mary McCarthy and Sidney Hook, would die before I had the chance to interview them. Many had long since stopped talking to one another, pulled apart by political and personal animosities, by geography, and by the changing habits of age. Yet as I interviewed them, each would ask for news of the others, envying me perhaps for my chance to freshly experience an era that existed for them now only as a kind of shadow world, an ever-present past that still could stir their passions.

Daniel Bell recalled a phone conversation he had had a few years earlier with Sidney Hook, then in his late eighties. Hook, once a vigorous man, had become frail, his voice quavering as he spoke from his home in California. And then Bell happened to mention Irving Howe, with whom Hook had had a lifelong political battle. Suddenly Hook's voice was transformed, his lungs became powerful, his words torrentially angry and disdainful. Bell later mentioned the conversation to Howe, who replied, "Well, if I can keep Sidney alive a little longer . . ."

When I interviewed the late Diana Trilling, she was eighty-eight years old. A proud woman bent by age, she was nearly blind at the time and working on *The Beginning of the Journey*, her memoir of her early life with her late husband, the literary critic Lionel Trilling. An inveterate rewriter, she composed the first draft with the aid of a large magnifying lamp tipped above her desk and employed a series of Columbia undergraduates as readers so that she might still rework her prose. She was suffering from emphysema and complained of her lack of stamina and ill health. Yet when she sat on the couch to talk about her life, the force of her voice and the strength of her formidable intellect kept her incandescently alight for two and a half hours. Who could believe that this was a woman who had to struggle for breath?

Engaging and prickly, she had a girlish flirtatiousness combined with a biting wit. When I showed her an old photograph of

Mary McCarthy—equally well known for her fierceness—cradling a cat in her arms, she perused the photo and glanced in my direction. "Who'll scratch first?" she slyly asked. Trilling had long been on a one-woman crusade to correct the misinterpretations of her husband's work and life that she seemed to discover in everything that had been written about him and the New York intellectuals. "I'm not going to believe anything I was ever taught," she told me, "because to judge by what is now being taught people about this century, they're not being told one word of truth!" Nevertheless, perhaps against her better judgment, she recounted for me her history.

Trilling memorably described the group's life as one of "significant contention." At first, when they remained relatively obscure—unlike their southern contemporaries, the group of New Critics that included Robert Penn Warren, John Crowe Ransom, and Allen Tate—William Phillips offered an explanation: "They're always praising one another and we're always attacking each other." But over time, it was, in fact, this argumentative quality that helped to bring them their enduring fame. If they were each distinguished by their individual accomplishments, and if the group as a whole gained recognition for its association with what William Barrett described as the two M's—Marxism and Modernism—they have more recently become an embodiment of a lost public intellectual life. The stuff of their arguments spilled onto the pages of their magazines in finely calibrated prose, making their endless conversation a running public discussion on everything that seemed to matter in the postwar years.

In later years, their very public opinions would provide fuel for the seemingly endless numbers of books written about them. Their own series of score-settling memoirs in turn provided a backward look at their highly charged, rancorous, and fascinating lives. Irving Howe in his classic 1968 essay, "The New York Intellectuals: A Chronicle and a Critique," in which he was the first to coin the term "New York intellectual," described the world of the former radicals as "closer to the vision of life we associate with Hobbes than with Kropotkin"—closer, that is, to a primeval world of brutal competition than to the anarchist's vision of an effortlessly harmonious social paradise!

They were always attacking one another; indeed, they made their careers out of it. Alfred Kazin described his fellow New York Intellectuals as "Critics with a capital C . . . first and foremost of each other." Daniel Bell recalls that the group "differed widely and sometimes savagely." In the forties, Diana Trilling remembered reading a sharp critique of a book she had admired. She asked the reviewer why he had not mentioned any of the book's positive qualities. "You don't expect me to review the good parts?!" he shouted at her incredulously. Nathan Glazer summed up the classic *Commentary* book review of the fifties as "Well, its not Tolstoy!" In *Armies of the Night*, Norman Mailer's at once self-lacerating and self-aggrandizing book about the anti–Vietnam War movement, he recalls strategically avoiding a friendly chat with Dwight Macdonald at a cocktail party for fear that Macdonald would consequently bend over backward to be tough on Mailer's latest book so as to disprove any possible charge of cronyism.

But the atmosphere of savagery and unending competition did not just produce wounds; it was the fertile environment in which grew a surprising amount of influential work. If they were Critics, well then they produced Criticism on art, literature, politics, and society. It was sweeping yet dense, difficult yet accessible. Particularly in their early days, their interest in the large statement, the all-encompassing generalization, could at times show a disregard for the intricate details of proof. As Nathan Glazer pointed out in a 1984 essay, "It was enough to be right on the main, the big and overwhelming point. The intellectuals of New York were right about Communism, they were also right about the importance of Modernism. And just as they had intellectual gifts that enabled them to say something pertinent about great international issues without any particular expertise in those issues, it also turned out they could say something pertinent about literature without the deep study engaged in by the traditional academics in the universities."

As Glazer goes on to explain, this knack for the important generalization could not last. "The old New York intellectual style of pronouncing judgments on a less than adequate knowledge in politics and literature could not survive: it was specialize or die." Many of them—like Glazer himself, and Howe, Kristol, and Bell—did become more specialized, as literary critics, political journalists, and sociologists. Still, the ambition to make the large, the profound statement was important and stayed with them even as their work matured. And that explains, in large part, the reason that succeeding generations of intellectuals have turned to them as models in an age when academic specialization and identity politics can seem to balkanize intellectual debate and promote a narrowness of thought.

"These were people," remembered Norman Podhoretz, the longtime editor of *Commentary*, "for whom ideas mattered more than almost anything else, in many cases, more than personal relations." At the same time, Podhoretz noted, "they were stuck with one another" because very few people shared either their interests or their background in the late forties and early fifties. Podhoretz has famously referred to them as "the family" and though in my own conversations with them most seemed to reject his characterization—in part because they disdain the sentiment behind it— they are all aware that the intellectual and social consanguinity they shared in their youth had produced an intimacy that they would never quite find again.

Though they were not all Jewish, they did have a particularly Jewish ethos. Caught between the immigrant world of their largely uneducated, working-class parents and a larger American culture just beginning to open itself to Jews, they were in a real sense rootless cosmopolitans. (Among the non-Jews, Mary McCarthy was a Catholic orphan from the West Coast, and Dwight Macdonald, though a Protestant Yale man, had bohemian predilections and an interest in radical politics that unmoored him from the world of his birth.) The Jewish members of the group never disowned their past—or their Jewishness—but they could no longer feel completely at home in their parents' world and did not feel at ease in gentile America. Like many Jews of his generation, Irving Kristol had his first exposure to "Americans" in the army during World War II. "The army, for me, was a very profound education," Kristol explained. "I was a New York Jewish kid. I didn't know anything about America, and I didn't know anything about most ordinary people." Kristol had enlisted in Chicago, where his wife, the historian Gertrude Himmelfarb, was getting her graduate degree, and ended up with a tough group of young men largely from Cicero, Illinois, which was, as he recalled, "Al Capone's hometown." It was a far cry from the streets of Brooklyn.

Thrown in upon themselves by both choice and circumstance, they fought and thrived. "Having ideas," explained William Phillips, "meant defending the ideas, promoting the ideas, arguing. We were always arguing with each other, but within certain premises, which made us a community." It was at once self-protective and incestuous, and yet intellectually wide-ranging. "The atmosphere of *Partisan Review*," explained Alfred Kazin, "was both exciting, because of the wealth of their interests, and insular because of the nature of these people themselves." For the fiftieth-anniversary issue of *Partisan Review* in 1984, Glazer surveyed the journal's articles over the years and found few that dealt openly with Jewish issues. "There were references to the fate of the Jews, perhaps even a translation of the work of a Hebrew or Yiddish writer. One felt, however, that Jewish topics entered only if they passed a test of universal significance. The Hebrew Bible, if it were discussed, was in terms of literary considerations. . . . Political issues of concern to Jews . . . would have to demonstrate a universal significance. Jewishness as such, in a word, was parochial." Elliot Cohen, Podhoretz's predecessor as editor of *Commentary*, pointedly described his magazine as the "Jewish version of *Partisan Review*."

*PR* had come into existence before the war, a product of the internationalist aspirations of a young group of intellectuals attempting to transcend the parochialism of Jewish immigrant life; *Commentary* was a product of an emerging postwar American-Jewish sensibility of nervous self-confidence, the result of the economic rise of the Jewish community combined with its continuing shock at the large-scale success of Hitler's war against the Jews. These factors made the idea of a *Jewish* magazine more legitimate in the eyes of mainstream Jews. (In the twenties, Cohen, a southern Jew from Alabama, had edited a much smaller Jewish magazine, the *Menorah Journal*, but it did not have the staying power of the later publication.) But even as a Jewish magazine, *Commentary* was assimilationist and, at least initially, opposed the Zionist aim of creating a Jewish state in Palestine.

In later years, their continuing reckoning with the Holocaust and the creation of the state of Israel would raise an awareness among the New York intellectuals of their Jewish identity. Israel's victory in the 1967 war would create tremendous pride in the American Jewish community as well as a lingering sense of the Jewish state's precarious existence. At home, the rise of the Black Power movement and the subsequent crumbling of the Black-Jewish civil rights coalition shattered their overwhelming faith and confidence in universalist goals. The ugly battle between black parents and the predominantly Jewish teachers union over community control of schools in the Ocean Hill–Brownsville section of Brooklyn led New York intellectuals like Norman Podhoretz to openly defend the interests of the Jewish community. Still, even as they became more openly involved in their Jewish identities, they could never shake their belief in a more expansive universalist agenda.

In recent years Daniel Bell has described himself as "Jewish in the fundamental sense that people always live in the tension between particularity and universal notions. If you're entirely universal, you become deracinated. You have no roots. If you're entirely particularized, you're rather narrowed by the orthodoxy of your creed and belief. So, it seems to me that my whole life has always been lived in that sense of the tension between the particular and the universal, at times, moving towards one or another pole." As a young student in elementary school, in fact, Bell had obliquely expressed his struggle with his identity in muffled words: "We'd go to school and we'd sing, 'My country 'tis of thee, sweet land of liberty, land where my fathers died,' and people would say, *Russia*. 'Land of the pilgrim's pride'—*Jerusalem*. 'From every mountainside'—*the Alps*."

In the film I did not have the opportunity to explore the changing Jewish identities of the four men. The film had begun as an examination of their political development, and these men were intellectuals who happened to be Jewish, not specifically Jewish intellectuals who focused primarily on Jewish issues. They were always conscious—and proud—of their Jewish heritage even as they wrestled with the inevitable contradictions that come from attempting to hold on to a secular Jewish identity in the modern world.

Glazer was the only one of the four at City College to belong to a Jewish radical group, Avukah, a peculiar blend of Zionism and revolutionary Marxism that could have flowered only in the radical thirties. As Glazer himself recently wrote of the group, "Our Zionism, we insisted, was pragmatic, flowing from an objective analysis of the political and economic position of the Jewish people, and divorced from any concern with its religion or its culture. We insisted on phrasing our concern for Jewish workers—not for Jews." His first book, however, was *American Judaism*, a sociological exploration of American Jewish religious practice, and perhaps his best known work, *Beyond the Melting Pot*, written with Daniel Patrick Moynihan, is a study of the importance of ethnicity in American life.

Irving Howe, the most staunchly secular of the four—so

much so that his City College classmate Seymour Martin Lipset was shocked to find him in synagogue for the High Holy Days late in his life—found his way back to his Jewish identity through Yiddish literature (he coedited five anthologies of translations) and ultimately through the book that would give him what he called his fifteen minutes of fame, *World of Our Fathers*, a brilliant study of the culture of Lower East Side immigrant Jewry. It is a book, however, by a lifelong socialist and literary critic that focuses on Jewish political radicalism and the arts rather than on religious practice.

Kristol, though never an observant Jew, found himself drawn to religious thought in general and Jewish theology in particular in the years after World War II. He was instrumental in initiating a Talmud study group that included himself, Glazer, and Bell. As a young child he was exposed to what he described as his parents' "decadent orthodoxy . . . where everyone observed, and no one believed, and no one cared. And no one read about it, and no one talked about it. They just observed." At *Commentary*, he was "the religion editor . . . since I was the only member of the staff who was really interested in what rabbis thought, so they'd give me the rabbis' articles to rewrite. Kristol's own interest in religion has remained perhaps more philosophical over the years, even as he has become a champion of religion as a source of meaning and structure in a modern world that often provides little of either. Today, he traces his own sense of ethics to the teachings of rabbinic Judaism with its sense of duties and obligations. Perhaps more than the other three men, Kristol is caught between his desire for religious belief and his innate dispassion for organized religious observance that dates back to his earliest years.

Between the first two generations of New York intellectuals—those that first gathered around *Partisan Review* in the thirties and those, like the four subjects of this book, who began to write for the magazine in the postwar years—there lay only ten to fifteen years' difference in age, and yet there remain critical differences between them.

While a strong interest in political ideas defined the group as a whole, the younger generation, seared by their early experience of the Great Depression, were, at their core, political beings in a way their elders were not. The initial *Partisan Review* group came to politics via art and literature: William Phillips and Philip Rahv were members of the Communist party's literary front for young writers, the John Reed Club; Lionel Trilling and his wife Diana were converted to Marxism at the artists' colony Yaddo by Sidney Hook. On the other hand, it was political radicalism that led Glazer, Bell, Kristol, and Howe to *Partisan Review* and to its interest in literary modernism. Kristol, like his friends, was enthralled with the magazine and often read its difficult articles over two or three times. "In twentieth-century literature and art," he recalls, "we ended up getting a much better education, I think, than most college students get these days, and it all began out of a political impulse."

Marxism initally offered them an ideological template to be laid out against the political and economic world that, they believed, would reveal the underlying meaning of its shapes and structures. As that map proved as much a distortion of American realities as a revelation of them, they found themselves grappling for new modes of understanding that were nevertheless infused with an appreciation for the subtle interrelationship between politics and culture developed in their radical youth. Even after their deradicalization, they continued to view the world through a political-cultural lens. It was just that the lens was no longer shaped according to Marxist principles.

Nathan Glazer can remember his sense of surprise the day Irving Howe first visited the offices of *Commentary* looking to do some book reviewing. At City College, Howe was perhaps the most unyieldingly political of all his friends, remembered as a budding Marxist theoretician who verged on the dogmatic, hardly someone whom the others imagined might flower into the brilliant literary critic he became. In part, his military service in Alaska during the war, far from the center of his radical world, provided him with ample time for literary reading to quell the routinized boredom of army life. Yet even as Howe gave up his life as a professional radical for the career of a critic, literature became a means, at least initially, of understanding his own political impulses through writers such as Ignazio Silone and Joseph Conrad. His first major work was the collection of essays that became *Politics and the Novel*.

For Bell and Glazer, socialism opened the door to the young discipline of sociology, which offered a rich, more intellectually flexible vehicle to study society. (Its relative youth also made sociology an easier entry point into the academy for Jews.) In addition to his work on ethnicity and American Jewry, Glazer produced a book, *The Social Basis of American Communism* (1961), which sought to understand who joined the Communist party and why. Bell's first book, *Marxian Socialism in the United States* (1952), was an attempt to understand the failure of the socialist movement (to which Bell had belonged) as a viable political alternative in America. Later he would try his hand at large-scale social theorizing, while Glazer would focus his efforts on the consequences of government social policy.

Kristol, though today the most overtly political of the group, was, in his early years, perhaps the least so, the last to join and earliest to defect from the radical movement. In the postwar years, Kristol, despite his misgivings about the "decadent religious orthodoxy" of his youth, gravitated toward an interest in literature and theology. Kristol found a set of intellectual and emotional impulses liberated by the study of theology and discovered in it a way to understand the large questions that Marxism had also proposed to answer. Kristol had earlier turned to the Protestant theologian Reinhold Niebuhr, himself a chastened man of the left, to help explain how the failures of socialism could be explained by a

Christian neo-orthodox sense of man's inherently flawed nature. When Kristol turned his interests once again to politics, his natural talent for political analysis expressed itself increasingly in ethical and moral concerns, not always the province of the political writer.

Ethical principles lay at the heart of each man's political philosophy, even as those philosophies evolved over the years in different directions. The four men fought not simply over political beliefs—the role of government in alleviating poverty or regulating public religious expression—but over ethical first principles as well. Liberals typically charge conservatives with mean-spiritedness toward the poor, and conservatives in turn see liberals as romantic do-gooders. The liberals charge the conservatives with lack of imagination, the conservatives in turn complain that liberals have an unrealistic excess of it. Howe derides Kristol as a "spokesman for corporate interests" and Kristol characterizes Howe's socialism as stemming from an ideological tradition so vague in its yearnings that it talks "about brave new worlds" with no real notion of how to create them.

After a lecture I gave on the film at a university last year, someone expressed shock that I spoke of Irving Kristol as if I respected his ideas! The remark was, at once, worthy of a New York intellectual and unjust to Kristol. After all, it had been my own somewhat surprised recognition that I could learn from a conservative thinker that had led to the making of the documentary, an experience I had hoped to place before the viewer. The New York intellectuals were deeply polemical, argumentative, at times inordinately critical of other viewpoints. Yet they always believed in arguing.

It was in argument that Bell, Glazer, Kristol, and Howe discovered the falseness of Stalinism, and it was through argument that they shed their own Marxist blinders. Kristol recalled that the City College years were a time of "internal self-examination. We were not just denouncing the bourgeois world or capitalism. In fact, we

really didn't spend that much time on it. It was much more interesting trying to figure out our own radicalism, and particularly
that absolutely overwhelming question that haunted us, namely,
was there something in Marxism and in Leninism that led to Stalinism?" Howe went on to point out that they "were raising some
of the most fundamental ethical and moral problems of politics,
but we wouldn't have put it that way. We had no awareness that we
were engaged in such lofty enterprises."

If *Arguing the World* is about the importance of intellectual
argument, it is also ultimately about the limitations of argument.
At City College in the thirties, the members of the Young Communist League were forbidden to talk with Trotskyists like Howe
and Kristol for fear of a kind of intellectual contamination. But
the members of alcove one could not help but goad their enemies
into debate. Howe remembers a fellow radical, somehow aptly
named Sammy Portnoy, who would hold a newspaper aloft scream-
ing, "Read about Stalin the butcher!" The shunning of argument,
of intellectual inquiry, by the Communist party—meant to bolster
its strength—ultimately proved to be a fatal weakness.

By the early fifties the enmity that had long separated the
former anti-Stalinist left—now liberal anti-Communists—from
the Communist left had been inflamed by McCarthy's anti-
Communist crusade. In the midst of official persecution of the
party, the four were still arguing with their old foes, pointing up
their penchant for secrecy and their unshakably naive faith in the
Soviet dictatorship. Bell and his friends felt that the Communists
before the congressional committees should have stood up to their
accusers, defending their beliefs rather than hiding behind the
Fifth and First amendments. And yet in the midst of the controversy, with careers on the line and families to support, it was not at
all clear that argument might have spared those who fought, and if
it had, it seemed a risky strategy to play against the manipulative
and unscrupulous tactics of McCarthy and his cohorts.

Confronted by the New Left in the sixties, the four men

found themselves unexpectedly arguing with a new generation of college radicals. Yet at every point argument was overwhelmed by animosity and incomprehension. For the New York intellectuals, argument had always been waged, as William Phillips noted, within "shared premises." And yet there seemed no common ground between the two generations, one reared by largely uneducated immigrant parents in the confines of Depression-era poverty and economic chaos who had, through hard work, carved out sucessful lives; the other floating lost in a world of affluence, searching for moral bearings in a country marked by increasingly impersonal bureaucracies, in the midst of an ambiguous and incompetently prosecuted war. Irving Howe and his *Dissent* group sat down with the young radicals of Students for a Democratic Society and fought over Communism. Nathan Glazer was initially proud of his students' fight for civil rights at Berkeley, but soon clashed with them over the role of political protest in the university. And Daniel Bell, frustrated by the demands of student protesters at Columbia, sought to argue with them even as the combined intransigence of the school administration and radical leaders finally erupted in a police riot on campus that left students bloodied and Bell himself in tears.

What, in the end, happened to the New York intellectuals? In many ways, they became the victims of their own success, the fabric of their world rent by forces both external and internal. The modernism they had championed for so long outside the academy became a staple of postwar culture, in large part through their own influential criticism and through the college courses they taught as newly minted professors. In the midst of the gigantic growth of the universites in the fifties, Glazer, Bell, and Howe had been invited to teach despite never having gotten their Ph.D.'s. In time Bell and Glazer would have degrees conferred on them, a belated recognition of the independent scholarship exhibited in their already published work.

Anti-Communism had, by this time, survived the legacy of McCarthyism and settled in as the unquestioned foreign policy of the Cold War years. The once-marginal political concerns of their avant-garde world had become the official ideology of mainstream America. These two intellectual causes, the twin poles that had served to define their existence as a group apart, could no longer hold them together.

If they saw the world differently, were less embattled, then America looked on them with new eyes as well. For so long they had lived their intellectual lives in their own small magazines: *Partisan Review*, *Commentary*, *The New Leader*, *Dissent*. And then came the day when others sought out their talents. Diana Trilling remembered that "something had happened in the culture . . . a homogenization of the culture so that people who edited the popular magazines, anything from *Good Housekeeping* to *Esquire*, could now call on the most serious writers and they were willing to write for those magazines and they had never been able to do this before." Irving Kristol recalled that "attitudes changed among the intellectuals of *Partisan Review*," who were once so disdainful of this "middlebrow" culture. "It turned out that they didn't want in, so long as they couldn't get in. But once they could get in, it turned out they didn't mind getting in!"

Suddenly without the need to hold together, the group inevitably succumbed to the centrifugal and ultimately polarizing forces of late-twentieth-century American politics. The self-searching initiated by their deradicalization led, over the next forty years, to diverging political paths. This process of change and evolution was abruptly catalyzed by the upheavals of the sixties. Friendships and political alliances were shattered, long-held political convictions finally came unmoored. The rise of the New Left and its impact on the Democratic party pushed Bell, Glazer, and Kristol to the rightward edge of the party's increasingly leftward politics. They fought for advancement based on strict merit as against affirmative action, they warned against the delegitimization of political authority and they feared growing and seemingly unquenchable economic demands placed on the government. The socialist Michael Harrington, an old ally of Irving Howe, nick-named them "neoconservatives."

But in fact, their individual trajectories over the next decade would prove too complex for the one-size-fits-all label. Irving Kris-tol supported Richard Nixon in 1972 and ultimately embraced the Republican party. He also, alone among his friends, gladly accepted the neoconservative title, famously quipping that a neo-conservative was "a liberal who had been mugged by reality." Bell and Glazer, however, did not vote for Nixon nor did they ever relinquish their identities as liberal critics of liberalism. Glazer was perhaps more pessimistic about liberal social programs and more willing to make common cause with conservatives, yet he never lost touch with liberalism and never relinquished his desire for lib-eral-minded programs for social and economic amelioration. Bell, more intent on distancing himself from conservatism, increasingly aimed his critical powers at the Republican party as its string of steady triumphs under Ronald Reagan and then Newt Gingrich made it a dominant political force.

Many have remarked on the discontinuity in the four men's lives: their break with their youthful radicalism in the postwar years and their loss of faith in the possibility of radical social change. It is true that their lives were not lived in a straight line; they did not tenaciously hold fast to the dreams of their youth. But to see only this about them is to miss the thread that can be traced for each one from youth to old age, a combination of per-sonal temperament and a set of intellectual interests that provide a continuity in Irving Kristol's political life as much as in Irving Howe's.

Among liberals there is a sense that Kristol has betrayed his former ideals, and yet this is a simplistic view of a man's life. At the age of twenty-three Kristol was writing for a small magazine called *Enquiry* that he, along with another City College friend,

Philip Selznick (later an eminent sociologist), had helped to found. Despite their youth, both young men were already skeptical refugees from Trotskyism. One of Kristol's articles for *Enquiry* critiqued Lionel Trilling's work and in its emphasis on moral values contains the seeds of Kristol's political and intellectual trajectory. In a recent autobiographical essay Kristol portrays his own political evolution as a kind of slow but inevitable process of self-revelation.

And beyond this, there is Irving Kristol, the man. His prose style, like his personality, is rooted in an intense passion, guarded by his ironic and often biting wit. Many have confused these, along with his stinging polemical style, for cynicism. But this error is founded on a misreading of the public posture, not the person.

Kristol's intelligence is expressed through a kind of epigrammatic skepticism ready to deflate overly grand social policy ideas. And yet he is a committed believer, a political warrior in many ways similar to Irving Howe despite their vast differences in temperament and style. Revealingly, it was Kristol and Michael Walzer, Howe's long time coeditor at *Dissent*, who separately expressed the need for a political program, Walzer explaining the need for "visions of radical transformation" as a means of keeping alive the idea "that social life is malleable." Kristol, in parallel terms, described the need for "a conservative agenda" because "with societies in flux, as they are, you do need an agenda to keep up with change."

Notoriously generous, Kristol has helped the careers of numerous young writers. The offices of *The Public Interest*, now in Washington, D.C., are small and plain, with largely unadorned white walls. The office contains two rooms, a larger one in which is arranged a horseshoe of desks where his young editorial staff sit facing a smaller office for Kristol and his assistant. There are no intervening doors and no individual offices, and this is the way Kristol likes it. His idea is to promote conversation and the flow of ideas among the staff, a system modeled on his alcove days at City

College. The young staff, dressed in white shirts and ties as one might imagine for the offices of a conservative publication, are thoughtful, intelligent young men and women. Kristol gives them Fridays off to read and write and think, always hoping to groom a new generation of intellectuals, but mischeviously notes that he loses many of his best and brightest to the more lucrative arena of law.

Glazer, his coeditor at *The Public Interest* and a professor emeritus of education and sociology at Harvard, has been typecast as a conservative by his opponents on the left, even while his ideas remain frustratingly unpredictable to many of his would-be allies on the right. He is a man willing to be openly, admittedly inconsistent, always measuring principle against its potential social consequences. After years of opposition to race-based affirmative action as an assault on merit, he has recently come to support such policies because their absence, in his eyes, would have a devastating effect on the numbers of African American students on elite college campuses.

Glazer is not only wary of political ideology, he seems immune to its temptations because he seeks no relief from the self-contradictions with which the complexity of life burdens us all. As an urbanist he has an infinite curiosity for the streets, neighborhoods, and people of the city. He is a man of the pavement, who has upended the role of the *flaneur*, turning aimless wandering into a purposeful and scholarly enterprise through his many essays on architecture and urban life. After an interview at City College, he insisted on forgoing a cab ride to his daughter's apartment so that he could take the subway, spending time at each of the stations along the forty-block journey to peruse the artwork that had recently been put on display.

At eighty, Daniel Bell is a surprisingly vigorous man who works in an upstairs office in his home in Cambridge. The office is small and has just enough room to hold his desk and an IBM Selectric typewriter. Bell, who has gained his substantial reputation writing about technology and its impact on society, still uses the machine for all of his writing, turning to his wife Pearl if any e-mail correspondence must be sent.

*Partisan Review* editor William Phillips described Bell as someone who "could read and write faster than I can talk." Now retired from Harvard, Bell recently joined with colleagues from Japan and Germany to found *Correspondence*, a journal that reports on international developments in the arts, culture, and politics. He has the temperament of a latter-day Enlightenment encyclopedist whose essays and books are stuffed with details and facts—he possesses an amazing memory that has tripped me up on several occasions—and yet he is a man who revels in the larger vision that only theory can illuminate.

Bell grew up speaking Yiddish on New York's Lower East Side and dreamed in Yiddish for many years; his language remains peppered with its words and phrases, his sense of humor inflected by the tradition of Yiddish storytelling. Often, in the midst of making a serious point, he'll suddenly veer off into a humorous anecdote—its punchline delivered with the perfect timing of a professional—to underline his meaning. Perhaps even more than his friends, Bell still retains the strong marks of his early Jewish education in *kheder*, the school where young boys study the Talmud. *Kheder* teaches one to think by contrary logic, to learn through argument, and Bell is an intellectual jouster who loves the give-and-take of intellectual battle and who remains, in many ways, the same young child—the smartie—who loved to challenge his teachers.

During my conversations with Irving Howe, his speech was leavened by a wry and self-deprecating sense of humor, yet he was remembered by friends and enemies alike as a ferocious debater, a skill he developed on the street corners of the Bronx and in the alcoves of City College. In his clashes with the New Left in the sixties, he was even known to make some of his young adversaries cry because of his ferocious debating style. He could be merciless with the naivete of his young antagonists, if he felt their ignorance of Communism was a danger to his beloved left. Cornered at Stanford University into less serious debate by a group of protesting students and frustrated at their attacks on his supposed lack of radicalism, he let loose with the ultimate put-down. He looked at one of his antagonists and yelled, "You know what you're going to end up? *A dentist!*"

At City College, he was a leader among the small group of Trotskyists to which he belonged and, apparently, a quite dogmatic theorist. His subsequent life in literature transformed him into a writer of great subtlety, a man whose mind searched out the untidy complexities that exist under the veil of pure theoretical abstractions. He worked in his home without benefit of a secretary and he was all business on the phone, as intently terse as he was voluble in person. In the few times I phoned him, as the conversation ended—which was usually quite quickly— there was rarely a good-bye, only the click of the receiver to announce that the conversation was over. I always assumed that I had somehow betrayed my ignorance. It was not until after his death that, in talking to one of the editors of *Dissent*, I learned that this was just Howe's way. In fact, the journal's young staff had a long-standing contest to see who might keep him on the phone the longest.

They are all extraordinary men and wonderful talkers, and in the pages that follow I cannot help but regret that you will not hear the timbre of their voices nor see their facial expressions. Even so, I console myself with the fact that I have been able to include here a great deal more of what they said during our conversations than was possible in the film. And as you read their words you will, I think, find revealed in them the same wonderful idiosyncrasies of their individual personalities, the passion of their speech, the strength of their language, and their unquenchable desire to argue with the world.

# 2. History at the Kitchen Table

GROWING UP IN THE JEWISH WORLD OF NEW YORK, EVEN THOUGH ONE
HAD RELIGIOUS EDUCATION, DID NOT MAKE ONE PRIMARILY RELIGIOUS,
IT MADE ONE MORE ALERT TO THE WORLD. IT WAS A KIND OF DOUBLE
CONSCIOUSNESS. WE'D GO TO SCHOOL AND WE'D SING "MY COUNTRY
'TIS OF THEE, SWEET LAND OF LIBERTY, LAND WHERE MY FATHERS
DIED," AND PEOPLE WOULD SAY, *RUSSIA*. "LAND OF THE PILGRIM'S
PRIDE"—*JERUSALEM*. "FROM EVERY MOUNTAINSIDE"—*THE ALPS*.

—*Daniel Bell*

HISTORICAL CONSCIOUSNESS WAS PART OF IMMIGRANT JEWISH LIFE.
THE IMMIGRANT JEWS BROUGHT WITH THEM MEMORIES OF THE OLD
COUNTRY, LEGENDS AND STORIES ABOUT THINGS THAT HAD HAPPENED
THERE, SO YOU ABSORBED THIS KIND OF HISTORICAL CONSCIOUSNESS
AT THE KITCHEN TABLE. LITERALLY AT THE KITCHEN TABLE. AND SO HIS-
TORY CAME TO ONE UNBIDDEN. IT WASN'T THAT I'D MADE THE DECI-
SION TO HAVE AN HISTORICAL CONSCIOUSNESS, IT WAS THAT HISTORI-
CAL CONSCIOUSNESS WAS PART OF MY ELEMENTAL LIFE, PART OF MY
NATURAL BEING IN THESE YEARS.

—*Irving Howe*

*Daniel Bell (b. 1919), Nathan Glazer (b. 1923), Irving Howe (1920–93),
and Irving Kristol (b. 1920) were all the sons of Eastern European Jewish
immigrants who had made their way to the United States in the great
wave of immigration beginning in the 1880s. By the twenties there were
close to two million Jews living in New York City, making the city nearly
one-third Jewish.*

*The immigrants had fled poverty and persecution in Europe; they sought in America not only the possibility of wealth, but the promise of political freedom. For centuries Jews had lived without political rights, isolated in small villages and shtetls, the local market towns where much of daily commerce was conducted. In Russia they were barred from living outside the western provinces that today comprise Poland, Lithuania, Belarus, and Ukraine, and which were collectively known at the time as the "Pale of Settlement."*

*Most immigrant Jews first settled on Manhattan's Lower East Side, where Daniel Bell grew up. A warren of cramped and barely heated tenements, it was also home to the city's poorest Jews. Successive legal reforms had required indoor toilets, heated water, and mandated windows in all rooms of the often airless and gloomy apartments. Outside, on the streets, the dense population produced a thriving Jewish commercial and cultural life: peddlers, small businessmen, a series of Yiddish newspapers, and a host of Yiddish theaters.*

*Even limited financial success allowed many immigrants to spread across the city in search of larger apartments. Their migration traced the outstretched tentacles of New York's expanding subway system north to the Bronx, where Irving Howe and Nathan Glazer lived, and east to Brooklyn, where Irving Kristol grew up. But even this meager prosperity was soon rendered precarious by the Great Depression that swept across the country as the four boys entered their teenage years.*

*For many immigrants, who often had few skills and little command of English, New York's garment industry provided a livelihood. Sweatshops employed huge numbers of men and women working long hours in dangerously overcrowded lofts. With their wooden floors, primitive electric wiring, and lack of exits, these factories were notoriously susceptible to fire. The most famous, the Triangle Shirtwaist fire of 1911, killled hundreds and catalyzed garment workers' unions into demanding safer working conditions.*

*In* World of Our Fathers, *Howe explains that "the job of putting together a single garment would be given to an operator, the needle work to a baster and a finisher, and minor tasks, such as sewing on buttons, felling, and pressing, to still others. In one leading garment shop in New York at the turn of the century, no fewer that thirty-nine tasks were carried on by the same number of workers in order to manufacture a single garment."* Bell's mother and Glazer's father became sewing machine operators, while Howe's parents worked as pressers. Smaller independent business-es run by middlemen, such as Irving Kristol's father, contracted out to perform parts of the labor-intensive process. The business, seasonal at best, could offer only an uncertain living to many families when the Depression struck.

## Daniel Bell

I grew up on the Lower East Side before the housing projects and before the highway. There used to be these long piers jutting out into the river. In the summertime, we used to swim between the piers. There were tin shacks along the docks where people lived. The garbage scows would tie up along the piers and people would go ransacking them for bits of food.

We used to go to the West Side fruit markets, which were under what is today the West Side Highway. I was then about twelve or so. At twelve o'clock at night the trucks would come rolling in with potatoes, lettuce, and tomatoes. And we'd make grabs. Somebody'd walk by and knock over a crate. The crate would break. We'd grab and run back.

My father died when I was an infant. We lived with an aunt—my mother, my brother, and myself in one bedroom. There'd be two beds. And there'd be two bedrooms for my aunt and uncle and their three children, and then a large kitchen. There was no such thing as a living room or a dining room, you simply ate and lived in the kitchen. There was a toilet in the hall.

The thing I remember best, curiously enough, about the tenement is how cold it was in the toilet in the wintertime. The hallway, the rooms—we'd never say "apartment"—would have the heat from the stove, but if you wanted to go to the toilet, it was cold. And the thing I always wanted was sweaters. (One of the things I have now is a large number of sweaters. I don't need them all, mind you. But if it's a nice sweater, I have to get it.)

In the wintertime, you lived in the staircases. It was cold outside, and therefore, everybody would congregate on the staircases, particularly kids. There were a lot of kids there.

In the summertime, older people would sit on the stoop; the kids would run around on the streets. It would be crowded. You'd have horses and wagons. My grandfather used to be on a horse and wagon; he would deliver ice in the summertime and coal in the wintertime, and I'd be with him. And the street would be full of shit, literally. So that you'd get those smells: urine, defecation, garbage.

There also used to be something called street singers, people who went to backyards and sang, and you'd take a couple of pennies and throw them down. They'd sing about five minutes, some melancholy song, and you'd throw down the pennies. These were Russian Jewish singers that came to the backyard, you see. Often people who couldn't get work in the Jewish theater.

My mother was a dressmaker. Our world was divided into slack and busy. I don't know whether you've ever heard that word, "slack." Slack is the season when nothing is there, and there's also the busy season. There were certain seasons where she'd be working eight, ten, twelve hours a day, and I would be put into what was then called a "day orphanage," but actually, quite often, I'd spend the night there because my mother couldn't come home in time to feed us. My elder brother would be with my grandparents, and they couldn't take care of both of us. I was called the *vilde*. I was the wild one. He was the more quiet one. So, my grandparents didn't want to have me in the house there, you see? So I would roam the streets.

After we left my aunt's house, we lived first in a backyard tenement. It was cheaper. As my mother got a little more money and saved some, we moved into another apartment in a front yard tenement. Often my mother would have a boarder. There were a lot of single males so the boarder would have one bedroom, we'd have the other. And by having a boarder, we'd be able to afford a [better] apartment. So I suppose this was the definition of upward mobility. A backyard tenement to a front yard tenement, to having a boarder so that you were able to afford to have some better places.

## Irving Kristol

We were poor, but then everyone was poor, more or less. When poverty is near universal in your universe, you don't experience it as poverty. Brooklyn was a mixture of Jews, Italians, Irish, and WASPS. It was a pretty good place to grow up in those days. Street crime was almost unheard of. There was no subway crime. I rode the subways morning, noon, and night. I used to play punchball in the street, and you'd wait for the trolleys to pass, because there were trolleys on the cow path even then.

We lived in a tenement—a walk-up—four or five floors. And of course it was small. So our rooms were very small, we had very few of them. I shared a bedroom with my sister for a while, I slept in the hall, then I slept in the dining room. It didn't matter, because everyone was doing that. The rooms, in fact, by today's standards would be extraordinarily small. And I'm sure the entire building would be condemned!

My mother was an elementary school graduate. That was regarded as educated in our family. My father never even went to elementary school. But he could read Yiddish, and he learned to read English. I don't know how he did it, but he did it.

He was a contractor, as they called it, in the men's clothing trade. He specialized in boy's clothing. And mainly, he got contracts from manufacturers of clothing, to cut it in a certain way, and prepare it in a certain way. And then send it back to the manufacturer for final finishing. He was a small businessman, went bankrupt several times. I remember my father breaking down and crying—and he wasn't the sort of man to do that—not in front of me, but when he thought I wasn't there because he had lost his job, or his business had gone bankrupt. He had to work as a cutter for a while. These were the Depression years. He actually prospered in the 1920s and he prospered in the 1940s. In between, it was very hard.

My mother died when I was sixteen. She had been ill for two years, with cancer. One of the things I did in those days—I was at Boys' High—was shopping for the family. On the way home from high school, I would stop off and I had a shopping list, and after a while, they all knew me in the shop.

I don't think I was really close to my mother. Being close to your parents wasn't really regarded as being all that important. Your parents were your parents and that's all there was to it. I'm amused to watch television shows these days where the parents go around hugging their kids saying, "I love you." I want to tell you, that never happened in the families I knew, in Brooklyn, in those days. You'd be embarrassed if one of your parents came up and said, "I love you." What are you supposed to say to that? No, but absolute trust. Absolute loyalty. Absolute commitment. And that's what family was.

## Nathan Glazer

I was born in East Harlem. My family had moved up from the Lower East Side just a year or two before I was born. There were nine of us after I was born, living in four rooms on East 103rd Street between Second and Third Avenue. And then we lived in another place in East Harlem, which was five rooms on East 97th. And then we moved to a six- or seven-room apartment on Kelly Street in the East Bronx.

When we finally moved, we were in way over our head at sixty dollars a month rent. On Kelly Street you could get six or seven rooms for less money. It was something like thirty-five dollars a month. The buildings had large apartments, and they would run six or seven rooms to the back, so you really could spread out.

We finally had a dining room. That was important. There were family gatherings there, the Friday night dinner, there were festival events like Passover. People would even have bar mitzvahs. Not that somebody wouldn't be sleeping there sometime.

My father was a garment worker, a sewing machine operator. He would specialize on coats for little girls. He generally worked at places called "Little Princess" and things like that. And when there was work, he worked. And when there wasn't, it was "slack." And there were good times and bad, though most of the thirties was very bad.

During most of the Depression, my father might work as little as a few months of the year. My mother didn't work. My oldest brother was often unemployed. He had gone to work at the age of twelve or thirteen as a Western Union messenger boy. The steadiest earners were my older sisters as secretaries. I think they probably did best in terms of jobs in the Depression. Of course, the younger ones like me were going to school. We were never exactly on welfare, but occasionally there'd be a message around, you could pick up free cans of vegetables somewhere—relief goods—and you could go down and get some of that. But generally we couldn't use them because it was pork and beans or something *trayf* [unkosher].

I have a picture of myself at five or six, an oval tin affair, painted, and I'm wearing a suit that my father had made for me—short pants, pockets, and so forth. We had a beautiful Singer sewing machine set in a wooden table with a cast iron base. That was used for making clothes for the family. He basically used it for repairs and for years, for example, he would turn collars for me. You know, when collars wore out. He was a very good collar turner, and since then, I've been throwing away shirts that were perfectly good, because who's going to turn a collar anymore?

## Irving Howe

My folks had a grocery store, it went bankrupt and they had to move in with my grandmother in a cramped apartment with many people. For many years I didn't have a room of my own. We were very close to destitution. We moved from the West Bronx to the East Bronx. That may seem like a trivial thing but it was a drop in social ascent. The West Bronx was the middle-class area, the East Bronx was the working-class area and for a kid of eleven or twelve the transition was very difficult and perplexing and painful. It was like having everything fall out from under you.

The thought of getting a job was something which no one really expected to be possible. The thought of a career or future was not something which one could live by. The expectation that one's parents could bring in enough money next week by which to live was very small. There was a sense of chaos, of disintegration. And so the socialist view, the radical view, seemed to bring to young people a total understanding. It wasn't fragmentary. It seemed to suggest a conceptual frame by which one could structure and give meaning to these very difficult experiences.

And so it was a very normal thing for a kid with some sort of introspectiveness and intellectuality, such as it was, to turn to politics And there was a group of Yipsels, Young People's Socialist League, a few blocks away from where I lived.

Especially in the immigrant Jewish neighborhood where I grew up in the east Bronx, politics was meat and drink. The political campaigns of 1932 and 1936 were very vigorous, very active. The Socialists mounted within their limited means a considerable campaign. The first time I heard Norman Thomas speak it was a thrilling experience. There was something pure and beautiful about this man's voice!

*In 1932 Norman Thomas—heir to the great Socialist leader Eugene V. Debs—won nearly a million votes in the presidential election, thanks in large part to strong support among Jewish immigrants and their children. "The answer to unemployment," he proclaimed, "is nothing less than worldwide socialism. The answer to the troubles that beset us is worldwide socialism. But on that road to that glorious goal, there are means we can do now, now to break the back of this misery, which rests like a curse on people in every hamlet, in every city and every town of America."*

*Turning away from centuries of religious belief, many young American Jews saw in socialism and its world-embracing vision a new and more powerful revelation. From the ravages of capitalism, a just society would be built. Working men and women would take their place as natural leaders of a new world, and among their ranks would be the sons of impoverished immigrants.*

## Daniel Bell

The *shul* and the Socialist party—that framed my life. When I had my bar mitzvah, I read my *haftorah*, [a selection from the Prophets read after the Torah]. And I said to the rabbi, I found the truth. I don't believe in God. I'll put on *tefillin* once, in the memory of my dead father, but that's all. I'm joining the Young Socialists League. The rabbi said, "*Yingle*"—kid—"you don't believe in God. Tell me, *you think God cares?*" Well, I was so angry at that, that he'd talk that way.

Coming out of an immigrant world, in which one's parents were preoccupied with making a living, preoccupied with day-to-day existence, who are not illiterate, but not basically cultured, and suddenly the world opens up, and this is what the socialist movement did for me. It suddenly shows there's a world of ideas, a world of experience, a world of imagination, so that, well, eagerly, you know, one becomes almost greedy in reaching for this.

*The socialist idea that inspired Daniel Bell and Irving Howe had first appeared more than a hundred years earlier. By the mid-nineteenth century Karl Marx, in his theory of "scientific socialism," claimed to have revealed the economic forces that shape history. Marxism predicted an inevitable clash between capitalist rich and poor that would ultimately bring the working class to power. His* Communist Manifesto, *published in 1848, was a workers' call to arms, but despite several aborted revolutions across Europe that year, no socialist group managed to gain lasting power.*

*And then in 1917, in the midst of war and revolution, Vladimir Lenin and his small band of Communists seized power in Russia in the name of the workers. The Russian Revolution resonated among socialists across the world. In America as in Europe, many broke from the Socialist party to create a new Communist party. Though the two quickly became fierce rivals, Lenin's triumph convinced both parties that Marxism was the answer and that a socialist state was destined to become reality in America, too. With the onset of the Great Depression in the early thirties, increasing numbers of men and women gravitated toward radicalism and huge crowds began turning out in New York's Union Square to celebrate the worker's holiday each May 1.*

## Lionel Abel
### Literary Critic

Those May Days were quite different from anything you see now. The police came out to do battle. The mounted police. And the masses of people who came to celebrate May Day called them cossacks. And there were young fellows, probably C.P.'ers, who wanted to fight with the police. So there was a lot of brutality. Grover Whalen, I think, was head of the police and he broke up the demonstration in '31, which I saw. And I saw a policeman run after a woman, with his club raised to strike her. She turned around and she said to him, "You're a slave!" At which he hit her and arrested her!

The Communists were the ones who presented what seemed to many a coherent explanation of joblessness, the rise of fascism, and the probability of war, of international war; that this was the worst crisis the capitalist system had endured, and that it wasn't possible to recover from it. And many were convinced by it. Not everyone, but then, you know, when people began to join, it becomes like the spread of an epidemic. It's a contagion.

## Daniel Bell

Socialism gave us answers to this world reading Marx, reading the *Communist Manifesto*, reading *Das Kapital*. And to that extent, it was a sense of hope. And you were able to take the same kind of reasoning, the same kind of thinking you learned in *kheder* [a school where young boys studied the Torah and Talmud] and now deal with real-world problems. So we'd read *Kapital* the same way we read *humash*, line by line. In *kheder* there was a great pressure to learn by a sort of contrary logic. The very first thing at *kheder* you read is the *humash*—the Torah—and you want to show the rabbi how smart you are. You say, "*Berayshit*,"—he'd say, "Wait a minute, wait a minute, wait a minute. What are you saying?"

And you'd say, "I'm repeating the first words of the *humash*." What's the first word? "*Berayshit*—'In the beginning.'" "What's God doing?" "He's beginning the world." "Well, God is not a capricious God. There must be reason for what he does. With what letter is he beginning? Why should God begin with the letter B?" So you suddenly begin thinking. Learning how to read is learning how to question. You're first taken aback, when you ask, Why should God begin with the letter B? One very rarely thinks of it. And yet, he's beginning the world. And then the *melamed* [teacher] would say, "Why not begin the world with the letter shin?" Which is how one of the names of God begins. Well *shin* also stands for *shav* which is "lie," and *sheker* which is "falsehood." So you can't begin the world so compromised.

Now, that kind of *pilpul* [debate] trains you, arms you to be anything you want. There's a title of a book by Issac Deutscher called *The Armed Prophet* about Trotsky, you see. And he meant that sort of revolutionary arming. But it really goes back to Jewish education. You're an armed prophet. Anything is assailable for you.

*Even those who were not politically active absorbed the radical atmosphere that permeated Jewish life through newspapers—such as the Communist* Freiheit *and the socialist* Forward*—and through the unions to which most garment workers belonged. The rivalry between Communists and Socialists played itself out in fierce fights for the allegiance of workers. Socialist unions like the International Ladies Garment Workers vied with those dominated by the Communists, such as the Fur and Leather Workers.*

## Nathan Glazer

I remember the presidential campaign of '32, because I discovered for the first time my father was a socialist. My mother had never gone to school, though she could read Yiddish and read the *Daily Forward*. My father had certainly not gone to any secular school. Maybe he had gone to a *kheder*. He voted for the Socialist party, and he was a member of the International Ladies Garment Workers Union. He was anti-Communist because he had been involved in the twenties in the struggle over the control of the union.

## Irving Kristol

My father was a union member. In those days, even if you were a boss, you became a member of the Amalgamated Clothing Workers. The Amalgamated Clothing Workers ran the whole industry, so you joined the union. In general, everything depended on what Yiddish newspaper you read.

## Daniel Bell

The crucial influence was the *Jewish Daily Forward*. This after all was the most powerful newspaper at the time. My mother read it—I was going to say religiously!—which is probably true. My mother herself was not political other than the fact that she voted Socialist. The *Forward* was a socialist paper. It was a Jewish socialist paper. My mother worked in a shop, and she was a member of the union. So the sense of union was very strong, and that was the Ladies Garment Workers Union. But there was always the paper.

## Irving Kristol

My sister was five years older than I was. She was influenced mainly by the Communists. And took out a subscription to *The New Masses*, which came into the house, which I read. And that helped radicalize me. And I remember, she took me to the theater. The first play I ever saw was *Tobacco Road* [by Erskine Caldwell], which is all about the terrible plight of the poor whites—not blacks—but poor whites in the South. I felt so much sympathy. There I was in Brooklyn, in what we would today call poverty, but all of my sympathy went out to the poor whites in the South. And the second play I ever saw was Clifford Odets's *Awake and Sing*, which I thought was absolutely marvelous. That was when I was around fifteen.

*Jewish radicalism burned with intensity, possessing an almost uncontain-able energy, its ideas bursting forth onto the streets of the immigrant neighborhoods. Soapbox orators—feverish visionaries—seemed to perch on every corner, holding forth for hours at a time.*

## Lionel Abel

The streets were filled with crowds listening to street speakers, and all these meetings were attended by people who would attack the speaker when he got finished, or ask him to answer questions, and there were often fights.

## Seymour Martin Lipset
## Member, Young People's Socialist League

The men used to be out in the parks in the West Bronx discussing politics. Fifty or so people standing around and maybe two or three people in the center, arguing, talking. Union Square was the proverbial place for this kind of debate. Sometimes somebody would set up a ladder and get up and people would come around. I can remember listening to Irving Howe speaking!

### Irving Howe

These were meetings which required no money, you just got a little stand and an American flag and you went to a corner—there were certain corners in the Bronx that we habitually used—and you would set up shop. We would try to sell a little bit of our literature, sometimes we would take up a collection. One would begin talking about the terrible conditions of life—unemployment, the threat of war, the problem of fascism and from there you went on. But mostly, it was a form of propaganda.

### Daniel Bell

The great slogan, of course, was "Socialism in Our Time." The idea was to preach ideology, to preach truth, to preach visions of justice, humanity, etc. And people would sometimes be skeptical, but sometimes they also would be eager to get these words. Because for most of them, the world was a drab, dreadful world. It was a problem getting something to eat. So you're trying to say in effect, No, there's a way out. And the way out was Socialist.

We weren't concerned about them voting Democratic or Republican, because we knew they wouldn't. They should vote Socialist, not Communist! That was the big problem, you see. And you always had to worry about the hecklers, who would say, "Why not vote Communist?" And you'd have to say, "Because the Communists were against the people!" and you'd throw out all sorts of arguments.

### Irving Howe

The essential thing for a street corner speaker is to work the back-and-forth relationship, the give and take, because the audience in a street corner is not one that just stands quietly. It participates. It joins in. It heckles. There was no great requirement that you be entirely coherent or that you have an organized structure. Those of my friends who spoke well, and some were quite brilliant at this, were able to achieve an emotional tie with the audience, were able to strike some chord in the feelings of the workers and the people who would gather around a street corner meeting. A good street corner speaker could go on for three quarters of an hour. I rarely lasted more than twenty minutes, even if that long. I had a certain gift. I could lose an audience in about three minutes.

## Daniel Bell

When I joined the Yipsels—this was 1932, Norman Thomas was running for president—a group of us would go from corner to corner with sort of a stepladder, and begin gathering a crowd until our main speaker would come along and talk. We needed some way of getting the crowds together. I was usually the first one up the ladder, and I had to speak for about ten minutes.

Well, you don't know very much when you're thirteen years old and you have to speak for ten minutes, so I pretty much memorized the last section of [Upton Sinclair's] *The Jungle*, which is Eugene Victor Debs's speech, and people would say, "How eloquent he is!" and there's nothing like that kind of applause and reinforcement to make you feel good, and I would sort of imitate the gestures of Debs, who would speak with his finger out. You've seen these pictures sometimes of Debs speaking, a long lean man with his finger out, and I'd lean out to the audience and people would sort of shrink back almost, and I'd pull them in.

## Nathan Glazer

The only thing I can remember is hearing a Republican speak. Imagine, a Republican in East Harlem in '32, and feeling a certain degree of sympathy for Herbert Hoover, and this was very surprising to me. Who had heard of a Republican, and who knew about Herbert Hoover's trials and tribulations?

What I knew was that Communists were not to be trusted. If you had asked me why that was, I don't think I would have known. It was simply being raised in a home where we accepted the evil of the Soviet regime, that terrible things were going on in Russia. How much I knew, I really just can't say. But I certainly learned about it very rapidly at City College!

# 3. A Harvard for the Poor

ALCOVE NO. 1 WAS LOCATED IN THE CITY COLLEGE LUNCHROOM, A
VAST GROUND-FLOOR SPACE WHICH EVEN WE, WHO CAME FROM SLUMS
OR NEAR-SLUMS, JUDGED TO BE AN ESPECIALLY SLUMMY AND SMELLY
PLACE. IT WAS THERE ONE ATE LUNCH, PLAYED PING-PONG (SOMETIMES
WITH A NET, SOMETIMES WITHOUT), PASSED THE TIME OF DAY BETWEEN
AND AFTER CLASSES, ARGUED INCESSANTLY, AND GENERALLY DEVOTED
ONESELF TO SOLVING THE ULTIMATE PROBLEMS OF THE HUMAN RACE.
THE PENULTIMATE PROBLEMS WE FIGURED COULD BE LEFT FOR OUR
DECLINING YEARS, AFTER WE HAD GRADUATED.

—*Irving Kristol*, Memoirs of a Trotskyist

THE BASIC MEMORY WAS THAT OF A SORT OF POLITICAL SANDBOX. THE
BASIC MEMORY WAS TUSSLES WITH THE OTHER RADICAL STUDENTS.

—*Daniel Bell*

*In the midst of the Great Depression, Daniel Bell, Irving Howe, Irving Kristol, and Nathan Glazer entered the City College of New York, a gateway to the wider world for the bright, ambitious sons of the city's Jewish immigrant poor. Swelling applications during the Depression made the all-male college more competitive than ever.*

*Though its faculty could boast only a few distinguished names, most prominent among them the philosopher Morris Raphael Cohen, its student body was perhaps equal to that of Harvard, though a good deal more radical.*

*By the time the four young men arrived, City College had gained notoriety for its students' left-wing politics. In 1933 an anti-ROTC demonstration provoked a confrontation between radicals and the school's starched and humorless president, Frederick Robinson. Attacking protesters with his umbrella, Robinson derided his impoverished student body as "guttersnipes."*

*The following year, Robinson foolishly invited a group of Italian students representing Benito Mussolini's fascist regime to speak at a campus assembly. The school's student council president—also a member of the Young Communist League—strode to the podium and welcomed "the tricked and enslaved students of Fascist Italy." A teacher grabbed him, pulling him from the stage, and a melee ensued. Dozens of students were suspended, and four were expelled. Demonstrations lasted for weeks afterward, attracting the notice of New York's newspapers and newsreel cameras. A twin-headed effigy of Robinson and Mussolini was burned. City College, dubbed "the little red schoolhouse" by the Hearst press, was now recognized as perhaps the most radical school in the nation. It was also one of the few colleges in New York City a smart but poor boy could afford to attend.*

## Irving Kristol
## Class of 1940

Like most people with some political consciousness in the thirties, I assumed the world was coming to an end—capitalism would fall apart, there would be a terrible world war that would devastate the universe, and there would be no point in preparing oneself for a profession. I knew absolutely nothing about City College. All I knew about it was that it was free. So, even though I had a very good high school record, I took it for granted always that I would go to City College, and I went.

## Daniel Bell
## Class of 1939

City College was always in the news, because of the radicalism of the students. Because of the very famous episode of the fascist students being greeted by the president of the college and the protests going on, the fights against ROTC. So one was constantly aware. In fact, one was much more aware of City College than of Columbia. Columbia was for the genteel. It was sort of out there. I never had a feeling of what Columbia was. Harvard was even much further out, but City College was very vivid and real.

### Alfred Kazin
### Class of 1935

It was an experience that was so deep, fundamental—physically, politically—that in some ways, it exhausted me before I could graduate. To be a poor Jewish kid at City College, to grow up in what was essentially a ghetto atmosphere was, as a matter of course, to seek an outlet, to seek some kind of transcendence.

### Irving Howe
### Class of 1940

I went with anticipation, and fear. Anticipation that it would be very exciting, that I might even learn something, though I didn't learn terribly much—that was my own fault—and fear. The fear that these professors would put one down, the fear that it would be more than I could cope with or manage. You must remember I was a kid, I was sixteen years old when I went to City College. On the one hand, I had visions of great political activity. On the other hand, I was afraid of differential and integral calculus and as it turned out I had very good reason to be afraid of it.

### Nathan Glazer
### Class of 1944

The alternative to City in those days was NYU, and the feeling was that that was where the kids went who were dumber and had more money. Everyone lived at home and came by subway. We thought City College was a school for smart kids, because we knew you needed an eighty-eight or a ninety average in your high school courses to enter.

Tuition and board at Columbia was about six hundred dollars.

You realize we're talking about '39 or '40. A hot dog with mustard was five cents and the subway was five cents, so you see that six hundred dollars was a lot of money. A twenty-dollar-a-week job was a good job. It seemed out of the question. You were aware that if you were considered left or radical, it probably wasn't a good idea. There was a whiff of anti-Semitism.

*Just twenty blocks south of City College, Columbia University saw itself as a training ground for the city's Protestant elite. Faced with growing numbers of qualified Jewish applicants, many of the children of Eastern European immigrants, the school instituted an unofficial Jewish quota. One anonymous administrator explained that these children of Jewish immigrants "lacking 'social advantages'" were not "particularly pleasant companions" for Columbia's "natural constituency." The college's few Jewish students tended to be wealthy, assimilated German Jews. Accordingly, Columbia's president, Nicholas Murray Butler, had made an arrangement to steer the poorer Jews uptown to City College, whose majestic neo-Gothic buildings belied the school's essential poverty.*

### Irving Howe
The atmosphere was dingy—the place needed a paint job, the teachers were overworked, many of them were mediocre. It wasn't a very distinguished faculty at all. There were a few brilliant teachers like the legendary Morris Cohen [but among the students] there was an atmosphere of perfervid, overly heated, overly excited intellectuality, because the radicalism of the moment was essentially abstract.

### Irving Kristol
It was a highly political atmosphere. Other campuses had comparable groups but they weren't nearly so diverse or so large. City College, because of the kinds of kids that went there, located in the middle of the city and I would guess at least eighty-five to ninety percent Jewish and therefore with political traditions. The entire

student body was to one degree or another political although most of them were passively political. But the active political types numbered in the hundreds.

*A vast, gloomy, and pungent room ringed by a series of alcoves, the college cafeteria was the center of the school's restless political life. With large oak tables often used for Ping-Pong, each alcove was a world unto itself, a headquarters to one of the college's student groups. Among these were a small group of radicals who gathered daily to argue over Stalin, the Soviet Union, and the ultimate meaning of the Russian Revolution.*

### Irving Howe

The alcoves were little divisions in the lunchroom, sort of shaped like a horseshoe, in which students could sit and eat their lunch and there was a table on which we could put political literature.

### Irving Kristol

There were probably about a dozen or so. And they were big enough to encompass a Ping-Pong table and there were benches along the wall. When you had free classes, it was the only place to go. There were no fraternity houses, there were no other opportunities that the college offered to sit down and talk to someone.

### Irving Howe

I had a device of checking in at the beginning of a class when a teacher took attendance, if you could imagine, and then slipping out to go to the bathroom and coming back at the end of the hour and meanwhile spending that hour in the alcove.

### Irving Kristol

It was pretty sordid, because practically everyone took along lunch. It was regarded as profligate to actually go out and buy lunch. And no one had the money anyway, so we all brown-bagged it. And we would sit there and eat lunch and talk.

## Seymour Martin Lipset
## Class of 1943

People would get up on these tables and make speeches, one alcove would start yelling at the other and one of the debates was about Trotsky's military leadership. One of the people who was listening was the head of the ROTC, some colonel, and it turned out he had been in Russia with the American expeditionary force and he testified to Trotsky's military prowess!

## Daniel Bell

We organized our own courses. We had Writing 100 and Barricades 202 and got in these arguments. Except for a few cases, one didn't respect one's teachers. A few cases they were very bright, particularly younger ones, but by and large most of the teachers were all dodos and we educated ourselves. It became a kind of—not Hyde Park per se, but essentially a *kheder*. It's a place where you constantly were disputing.

## Nathan Glazer

We argued all the time. All the time. One of the chief things we had to weigh in our arguments was *The New York Times*. As in the expression, "Even *The New York Times* admits or asserts or says." *The Times* was the final authority.

## Philip Selznick
## Class of 1938

We used to use a phrase, "having a discussion." "Having a discussion" meant something rather special in those days. It meant a fairly passionate interchange, arguing about some factual matter or an interpretation or what have you and doing it at the top of your lungs! That was a discussion!

## Irving Kristol

Every alcove had its own identity, there was the jock alcove for the athletes. There were alcoves for the ROTC people—I don't think

I ever met one—and then there was the Catholic alcove, the Newman Club. I don't think I ever met one of those either. We did ghettoize ourselves. There was even, I am told, a Young Republican Club, but I don't think I met anyone who belonged to that club and maybe they didn't exist. But pretty much our life in City College was concentrated between alcove one and alcove two, the anti-Stalinist left and the Stalinist left. And that was our world, at least our intellectual universe.

*At City College, Kristol and Howe had found an intellectual hero in the exiled Soviet revolutionary Leon Trotsky. The Trotskyists gathered in alcove one with their radical cohorts, including socialists like Daniel Bell and radical Zionists like Nathan Glazer, who would join the alcove in a few years. And there was a host of tiny splinter groups, each with its own arcane gospel of theory and usually identified by the name of its dissident leader.*

## Irving Kristol

I had a couple of very good friends who had come with me from Boys' High to City College, and they had been influenced by the Trotskyists, who were a tiny group compared to the Communists, a quite large group. And I wanted to be a radical. In 1936–37, what else was there to be? So I decided to go along with the Trotskyists; there couldn't have been more than twelve.

Then you had some independents, another ten or so, and then you had small so-called splinter groups like the Lovestonites, and each of them maintained their radical purity as against what they regarded as the heresies of the other groups.

## Daniel Bell

You had Social Democrats or Socialists like myself. You had Lovestonite splinter groups. You had Marlinites, Ohlerites, Stamites. Names that are dimly lost in the footnote histories of the past.

## Nathan Glazer

In my first year I was taken to a meeting, was deeply impressed, and it was a student Zionist group. I had no particular Zionist leanings and I came from a home that was not Zionist. But a friend dragged me off to a meeting where City College alumnus Seymour Melman was going to talk about his year in Palestine, as it was then called. I went to speak to him after the meeting and he was always engaged in finding recruits. The next thing I knew I was editor of the student newspaper *Avukah Student Action!* Why he saw a potential editor in me I don't know. But I was rapidly swept up in the group.

It had a double character: as the student Zionist organization for those groups from the Midwest who were primarily Zionist and then as a Marxist Zionist organization for members from the New York area. It introduced me to sophisticated leftist thought and the whole history of Zionism. It was very left, very close to the Trotskyites on campus and to the anti–Communist left. And that brought me into the anti–Communist left group.

*The radicals of alcove one spent their days immersing themselves in radical theory, studying together the classic Marxist texts. In addition to Marx's own work, including his massive dissection of capitalism,* Das Kapital, *there was the work of his collaborator, Friedrich Engels, and of the German revolutionary Rosa Luxemburg, among others. And then there were those works that had sprung up in the midst of the Soviet revolution: books by Lenin, by Trotsky, and by other key revolutionaries such as Nikolai Bukharin.*

## Philip Selznick

You were simply plunging yourself into the literature to acquaint yourself with its nuances to make sure that you now are developing the expertise to be able to read the newspapers, and to come up with an interpretation of events, what we used to call a party line, the official position. That official position had to be thought out. There had to be an argument. And the capacity to make that argument and the capacity to bring to bear relevant facts and history and so on, this was a situation much to be desired from the point of view of your own self-image, self-respect.

## Nathan Glazer

Each of these groups would tend to gather to read what they felt to be the classics of their faction. But, first of all, we would read Marx, and I remember one of the first things Seymour Melman gave me, feeling I had to be educated as a Social Democrat, was Marx's *Wage-Labor and Capital*. It was like a forty- to sixty-page pamphlet and it was very enlightening, a good summary. In fact, I think possibly that's all one needs! And I know we read Nikolai Bukharin, his book, *Historical Materialism*.

## Daniel Bell

We'd read *Kapital*. And there was always the great sense of competitiveness of being able to cite a better source than somebody else. We'd be reading Engels on street tactics. We'd say, but comrades, there are no longer any paving blocks here, as in Paris. We can't dig up the paving blocks and throw them at the troops. What do we do? Ah! Real problems! And somebody would come up, of course, with a great solution. You'd be surprised how many great military strategists came out of City College! Somebody'd come up and say, well, if you can't get paving blocks and throw them at troops, you barricade each end of the street when the police are in there, and the brave revolutionary women—it's always the women who were given those tasks—the brave revolutionary women go up on top of the roof and throw down hot water!

## Irving Kristol

There were a lot of arguments of a highly Jesuitical nature. You would find a quotation from Trotsky or from Rosa Luxemburg and you would pose it as the text for the day and then you would argue about it. And this required knowing a lot about the Soviet Union, and we read a lot about the Soviet Union. This required knowing a lot about the history of the Communist movement and we read a lot about the history of the Communist movement—the international, not the American Communist movement. The discussions were really quite sophisticated. Looking back on it, pointless, but nevertheless sophisticated and good intellectual exercise.

### Daniel Bell

The great crushing rejoinder was in the end: Look, *you* know what Trotsky has to do and *I* know what Trotsky has to do, but does Trotsky know what he has to do?!

*Argumentative, contentious, divided in their beliefs, the boys of alcove one were united solely by their opposition to Soviet leader Joseph Stalin and to his much larger group of followers who had made their home next door in alcove two.*

### Daniel Bell

It was all a kind of defensive alliance against the Communists. That's what brings people together more often than not. And in City College this was the thing that counted.

### Irving Howe

Anyone who was an anti-Stalinist on the left was a natural ally for our beleaguered group, because we were distinctly—in the left-wing world at City College—a quite small minority and we felt, in fact we were, beleaguered. I would say in alcove one, which was the hangout of the various anti-Stalinist left groups, there may have been a total of fifty students. In alcove two, which was the hangout for Communist students, I would guess that they had upwards of four hundred to five hundred members, which was of course a very good deal.

At a certain point, I think it was '38 or '39, the Communists decided to break off all verbal relations with their opponents in alcove one, because we were steadily chipping away, taking away a few of their people, not very many but a few and some of the better, brighter ones.

## Irving Kristol

Members of the Young Communist League were forbidden to talk to us, I mean, literally forbidden by their organization to have a conversation!

## Seymour Martin Lipset

As far as the Communists were concerned the Trotskyists were not only traitors, they were fascists. They had a policy that no Communists were supposed to talk to a Trotskyist or debate them. They *could* talk to socialists.

## Irving Howe

We taunted them. We had one fellow with a foghorn voice named Sammy Portnoy, and he would stand in alcove one and hold up a socialist paper, a left-wing paper and yell, "Read about Stalin the Butcher," and they would become very aggravated and aroused and sometimes we would literally provoke them into entering a debate or discussion. Well, when that happened, we were usually better at this. They were better at many other things, they were better at taking over the student government, at organization, but we were quick on our feet intellectually, we were quick verbally, and we would taunt them into a debate and go at it.

## Nathan Glazer

I recall one story of a debate, between Seymour Melman and the Communists. Melman held forth for something like six or eight hours as various people rose up against him, then had to go to class! He decided to drop his classes, I suppose. And people would

come, and go to class, and come back, and he was still holding
forth, he was still going hammer and tongs. He had tremendous
energy. That was the old style, the style in which someone could
speak for three or four hours.

*The fight over Stalin had agitated radical circles for years. Stories highly
critical of the regime had filtered out of the Soviet Union; there were claims
of labor camps, political executions, and forced starvation. Did economic justice and political equality actually exist in the country that claimed to be
the world's first "worker's state"? From his exile in Mexico, Trotsky derided Stalin as a ruthless dictator bent on destroying all political opposition.*

*In 1936 a series of show trials began in Moscow. Over the course of
three years, many of the Soviet elite were accused of conspiring to under-
mine the revolution, in league with Nazi Germany. One after another,
they pleaded guilty to charges of foreign espionage and were executed. Trotsky himself was sentenced to death in absentia.*

*American Communists and their supporters among the intelligentsia,
like Walter Duranty of* The New York Times *and Malcolm Cowley of*
The New Republic, *rose to defend the trials. But for the anti-Stalinist
left, the Moscow trials raised alarming new questions about the world's
first socialist state.*

*Lenin had made the Communist party a political weapon to rule
Russia, and Stalin had turned that weapon into an instrument of his own
personal power. Faced with Stalin's brutal regime, some began openly to
wonder whether Lenin's revolution had inevitably led to Stalin.*

### Philip Selznick

The experience of the Moscow trials with the revolution turning
upon its founders was a dramatic case, which many of us thought
about a great deal, what was the larger significance of all of this,
what did it mean for the basic perspective of revolutionary Socialism, of Leninism?

I think that many of the ideas that we developed were largely
worked out, at some level at least, in response to those highly trau-

matic experiences. It wasn't just that some tyranny had been established, but that this tyranny arose out of the movement which was supposed to bring social justice to the world. That was the great contradiction with which we had to cope.

## Daniel Bell

Here were all the major figures who had created the Russian Revolution being murdered by Stalin. Not only being murdered, but being forced in an abject way to confess to the most ludicrous kinds of accusations: that they were agents of the Gestapo, agents of Germany, etc. These were people, many of them who had a certain kind of aura. Zinoviev had been the head of the Communist International; Bukharin had been the editor of *Pravda* [the Soviet party newspaper], and he had written the main textbook called *Historical Materialism*. You had a situation where the entire group of revolutionary persons, almost without exception, was simply destroyed and forced in this way to bend the knee. And there just wasn't one set of trials, but a series of two or three and this went on over a period of several years. Plus of course the accusations against Trotsky that he had been the mastermind of the whole thing.

It was all captured in the old phrase: the Revolution devours its children. Here you had a situation wherein the Moscow trials in a personal, dramatic sense meant the revolution devouring its children.

There's a pamphlet of Rosa Luxemburg which a few of us knew. She said the dictatorship of the proletariat becomes the dictatorship of the party becomes the dictatorship of a single person. So there was a feeling all along that here was a regime which was no longer a regime of morality, a regime of hope.

## Irving Howe

We were raising some of the most fundamental ethical and moral problems of politics, though we wouldn't have put it that way. We had no awareness that we were engaged in such lofty enterprises.

We thought we were discussing revolutionary or Marxist strategy. At that point we thought of ourselves as anti-Stalinist Marxists, anti-Stalinist leftists. But as I see it now, we were often engaged in more fundamental, ethical questions. The whole problem of the nature of Stalinism. I put it now in abstract terms but that was really what we were talking about. The anti-Stalinist groups, which meant in those days mostly the Trotskyist youth group and the socialists and a few other left-wing groups, the main contribution they made politically, intellectually was in the fight against Stalinism and the fight against the totalitarian perversion that we saw Stalinism to mean.

### Irving Kristol

One of the reasons intellectual life in alcove one was so interesting was that so much of it was internal self-examination. We were not just denouncing the bourgeois world or capitalism. In fact, we really didn't spend that much time on it. It was much more interesting trying to figure out our own radicalism, and particularly that absolutely overwhelming question that haunted us, namely, was there something in Marxism and in Leninism that led to Stalinism? To what degree was there a connection? This was the question that all along bothered us, that was a prelude to our future politics.

### Irving Howe

Some of the particular theories we had about Stalinism have proven to be questionable, but in our insistence that any socialist value that was worth preserving had to be based on democracy, that socialism and democracy were indissoluble, there I think we were right.

### Irving Kristol

Irving Howe oddly enough at that time was the party boss of the Trotskyists. He was the one looked to for the authoritative doctrine on whatever the issue of the day was. He was the man who applied his mind to a rigorous definition of what was right and what was wrong in radical politics. I, myself, had not joined the Young Trotskyists until shortly after I left college, but I had been a fellow traveler for about three years. If anyone recruited me, I suppose you could say it was Irving Howe. He recruited me, one might say, and he also expelled me, about a year later, for coming to the conclusion that, in fact, there was an organic connection between Leninism and Stalinism.

## Irving Howe

I made a big mistake with Irving Kristol, and that was recruiting him to begin with. He wasn't, let's say, good material, but he wasn't expelled ever. He was part of a little group which developed different ideas, dissident ideas, and they left. When he called me the party boss or the chief ideologist he is perhaps transposing his own experiences in the Republican party in recent years to an earlier time. I suppose I and one or two others were the leading spokesmen, the most articulate figures around alcove one. But the organization of these groups was very loose. There was no effort at any kind of political or intellectual discipline. People spoke freely. We were Democrats, without recognizing it or acknowledging it, I believe. There was no effort to conform to a party line. If I was a party boss I don't know who I bossed around.

## Seymour Martin Lipset

If you joined the Trotskyist Yipsels, you were supposed to have a party name and mine was Lewis. The party name tradition went back to Russia, the Bolsheviks hiding from the Secret Police, confusing them. So the Communists all had party names, the Trotskyists all had party names, the Socialists didn't. Peter Rossi, the only guy I ever recruited for the movement, was Italian and came from Corona in Queens. He chose the party name Rosen. Well here we had one real gentile, a real *goy*, and he wanted to be called Rosen!

So Howe took it on himself to tell him that he should use another name, not a Jewish name.

Kristol became Ferry, his friend Earl Raab was Perry. Why? James P. Cannon, who was the leader of the Trotskyists, used to pronounce periphery, "perryferry." He'd talk about the "perryferry" of the movement. Kristol and Raab didn't join for a long time, but they were hanging around so they were on the periphery. They were the "perryferry." And when they joined they took the names Perry and Ferry!

## Daniel Bell

Howe at that time was still not Howe. He originally was Hornstein, Irving Hornstein. When I first knew him, curiously enough, he was using a very different name. He used a name called Hugh Ivan. He was writing polemical articles, so he used the name Hugh Ivan as a kind of Party name. So we argued at that time and became friends.

Curiosity led us to want to explore everything, know everything, be able to talk on everything. I suppose that's the definition of a New York intellectual: a man who given two minutes' preparation can speak for fifteen minutes on any subject in the world.

# 4. The Most Interesting Place in the Soviet Union

POLITICALLY, NEW YORK CITY THEN BECAME THE MOST INTERESTING PART OF THE SOVIET UNION, FOR IT BECAME THE ONE PART OF THAT COUNTRY IN WHICH THE STRUGGLE BETWEEN STALIN AND TROTSKY COULD BE OPENLY EXPRESSED, AND WAS, AND HOW. . . . LET IT BE NOTED, THE MOVEMENT OF THE CITY INTO THE USSR WAS UNPRECEDENTED AND UNDUPLICATED. NO OTHER GREAT CITY FOLLOWED NEW YORK. LONDON DID NOT; NOR DID PARIS. AND THESE WERE THE ADVANCED CITIES OF THE WORLD.

—*Lionel Abel,* New York City: A Remembrance

[UNION SQUARE] WAS COMMUNIST TERRITORY; "THEY" WERE EVERYWHERE—IN THE STREETS, IN THE CAFETERIAS; NEARLY EVERY DERELICT BUILDING CONTAINED AT LEAST ONE OF THEIR FRONT GROUPS OR SCHOOLS OR PUBLICATIONS. LATER, WHEN [*PARTISAN REVIEW*] MOVED TO THE OLD BIBLE HOUSE ON ASTOR PLACE, *THE NEW MASSES* HAD OFFICES ON THE SAME FLOOR AND MEETING "THEM" IN THE ELEVATORS, RIDING DOWN IN SILENCE, ENDURING THEIR COLD SCRUTINY, WAS A PROSPECT JOKED ABOUT BUT DREADED.

— *Mary McCarthy,* Theater Chronicles

*The anti-Stalinist left at City College watched with growing concern as fascism swept through Europe. After a three-year civil war from 1936 to 1939, Spain fell under Francisco Franco's dictatorship, following Benito Mussolini's ascension in Italy and Adolf Hitler's rise to power in Germany. In 1935, under this rising threat, Soviet leader Joseph Stalin directed Communist parties across the world to form alliances with those groups on the left the Communists had previously shunned. The era of the Popular Front had begun.*

*Shedding its revolutionary image and its sectarian politics, the American Communist party startlingly declared, in party chief Earl Browder's words, that "Communism is twentieth-century Americanism." The party soon embraced Franklin Roosevelt and his New Deal reforms.*

*The American Communist party created a vast number of "front" groups from the League Against War and Fascism to the League of American Writers, attracting thousands of often unsuspecting "fellow travelers" to the Communist cause. Despite its friendlier image and its growing popularity on the left, however, the Communist party remained firmly in the control of Soviet leader Joseph Stalin.*

### Diana Trilling
### Contributor, *Partisan Review*

I cannot exaggerate the part that fellow traveling, Communist fellow traveling, played in the culture of this country, in the thirties and even into the forties. It is not to be exaggerated. All the magazines, the artists, the musicians, the clergy, schoolteachers, students, all were organized by the Communist party, and the Communist party had a ready field from which to pick people. The whole culture, the whole intellectual culture.

I'm now talking about Stalin's Communism; I'm talking about the most totalitarian and repressive phase of Soviet history. And they had this incredible power to propagandize.

### Irving Howe

You had constantly during the Popular Front a difficulty that some of the things the Communists were proposing [like the united opposition to Hitler] made sense intrinsically, but their own manipulative demagogic authoritarianism alloyed and destroyed these policies. All the way through in the Popular Front period, the question of Communist manipulation and Communist domination—Communist bad faith—was a central problem.

## Diana Trilling

I've discovered that people who aren't of my generation or the next generation, at least, after mine, don't know what an innocent's club was. Had you ever heard the phrase? An innocent's club is the same as a front organization. You know, they take in the innocents and they lead them in the way of the party, but they never know that they're being led. And they don't know that they're serving a Communist cause; they think they're serving a liberal cause. There must have been dozens of them. They were all over the place.

## Irving Kristol

The non-Stalinist left found the Popular Front extraordinarily sickening, rather nauseating. The Communists turning on a dime, suddenly becoming pro-American at the behest of Moscow. We were internationalists, revolutionary internationalists.

*Vastly outnumbered by the Communists and their Popular Front supporters, the radicals of alcove one found themselves a beleaguered if vocal minority at City College. But their beliefs were echoed by a group of young Greenwich Village intellectuals equally isolated in the midst of the Popular Front's overwhelming influence among artists and writers.*

*The group was centered around the militantly anti-Stalinist journal* Partisan Review, *which was dedicated to combining literary modernism with Marxist politics.* PR *published T. S. Eliot's* The Dry Salvages *and* East Coker *as well as poems by Wallace Stevens, William Carlos Williams, John Berryman, W. H. Auden, and Marianne Moore; a London letter from George Orwell; pieces by Andre Gide, John Dos Passos; literary critic Edmund Wilson on "Flaubert's Politics"; Pablo Picasso on "The Dreams and Lies of Franco"; and even contributions from exiled Soviet leader Leon Trotsky himself.*

## Nathan Glazer

I'd never heard of *Partisan Review* before I went to City College, and the first issue of *Partisan Review* I ever saw was in Seymour

Melman's hands, and I said, "What's that?" And he said, "*Oh, this is very important. You have to read this.*" You know, that's the way we talked.

## Irving Howe

The Stalinists were middlebrow, the Trotskyists were highbrow, because they thought in the kind of terms that you had when *Partisan Review* started coming out, the union of two avant gardes, a political avant garde and a cultural avant garde. We prided ourselves on reading Joyce and Thomas Mann and Proust, maybe not completely, but at least dipping in, whereas they were reading palookas like Howard Fast.

## Lionel Abel
## Contributor, *Partisan Review*

*Partisan Review* established a connection between a different view of the Communist movement, one not known elsewhere, or not widely known, and literature. It provided a bridge between leftist views that were not orthodox, and literary reviews that were not orthodox, or that were experimental. So it related culture to a left-wing politics, which was different from the C.P.'s. And this was a very important cultural and political fact.

## Diana Trilling

It was a Marxist journal and yet it was a very avant garde journal in the arts. It was very extraordinary to find a magazine and group of people who shared one's left-wing anti-Communism, one's, if I may put it that way, one's advanced notions about books and the arts and also one's anti-Communism. This was a very, very extraordinary thing.

*Still in their twenties, the* Partisan Review *circle of writers had coalesced over a number of years. The magazine's chief editors, William Phillips and Philip Rahv, were disaffected Communists who had met in the party's*

*John Reed literary club and had begun the magazine under its auspices. Phillips was a City College alumnus, taking graduate courses at New York University; Rahv was a largely self-taught man who had emigrated from Russia at the age of fourteen. Impoverished by the Depression, Rahv had been forced, at times, to sleep on park benches while steeping himself in left-wing philosophy and modernist literature.*

## William Phillips
### Editor, *Partisan Review*

Modernism is hard to define. What it meant to us at the time, though was fairly concrete. What we meant was the kind of sophisticated and experimental writing and the kind of profound and radical consciousness that was exemplified, for example, in the works of writers like Kafka and Mann and Proust and Joyce and of course of many lesser figures.

It was the writing that expressed the sensibility of existence at that time. The Communists called it bourgeois writing and were against it and attacked us and were suspicious of Rahv and myself for leaning in that direction even before we broke completely. That indicated to us that the Communists were really not concerned with contemporary consciousness and contemporary existence.

## Lionel Abel

The thing one never forgot was that Phillips and Rahv were together. They were like a married couple. They wrote articles together, which seemed inconceivable to me, why anybody would want to share the writing of an article with anybody else. And there was another fellow around, then, who was a friend, James Farrell, who was a nationally known writer. We all looked up to him, and liked him. And he would always make fun of them. He called them Form and Content. And he'd say, "Have you been seeing Form and Content? What are they doing?" Because he thought it was funny, too, for two people to write, you know, on the same subject. Harold Rosenberg even called them Rosencrantz and Guildenstern.

### Diana Trilling

I think that probably Philip gave much more of the fiber to the magazine and that William gave amenity to the magazine, such as it was. They both had a kind of elegance. William's is the elegance of an intellectual and Philip Rahv's was a brutish elegance. He was a very big burly person and very stony-faced. He was like a character out of a Dostoevski novel. I think he would have liked being thought that. Whereas William was not ever, ever, ever a character out of a Dostoevski novel, he's very hypochondriacal, very worried about the proprieties.

### William Phillips

Rahv was basically, I suppose, a rhetorician—his life was composed of rhetoric. He was always arguing, and always in a loud voice, and always yelling, and always trying to knock down somebody else. I once called him a "manic impressive." Women were interested in Rahv because they thought he was Genghis Khan, ready to knock everybody over, you know, conquer everybody.

Rahv was a member of the Communist party. I was not a member of the party, but I was very close. I veered toward the John Reed Clubs—I think it was about 1932. I first met Rahv there. And I recognized that kind of kindred interest in radical ideas.

*If the boys of City College had discovered literature as a result of their politics, the group of writers around* Partisan Review *found their way to revolutionary politics through their love of literature. The Communist party courted writers as a means of propagandizing for its cause. Its John Reed Clubs were designed to attract young would-be writers like Phillips and Rahv while its literary journal,* The New Masses, *published party-approved and politically "correct" fiction and criticism.*

*Sidney Hook, a brilliant young philosopher at New York University, and a former teacher of William Phillips, proved enormously important in proselytizing for Marxism. In 1933, Hook, a protégé of the philosopher John Dewey, published* Towards an Understanding of Karl Marx, *in which he attempted to synthesize Dewey's pragmatism with Marxist theory. The book and its author became instantly influential. While never a party member himself, Hook early on supported the Communist cause, traveling to the Soviet Union to do research at the newly created Marx-Engels Institute. He would become a guiding political presence for the* Partisan Review *circle and its editors. Diana Trilling and her husband, Lionel, a professor of literature at Columbia, first met Hook at Yaddo, a writers' colony in upstate New York.*

## Diana Trilling

In the summer of 1931, Lionel was invited to Yaddo. And I was "invited," I suppose, in quotation marks—to trail along with him. There were about sixteen people and among them was Sidney Hook, who was then a young professor of philosophy, at NYU. One had heard of Sidney Hook, already; he was very, very brilliant. He had been a student of John Dewey's. A very gifted student of Morris Cohen, at City College. And he was a rising star in philosophy. He had just become a Marxist. And he converted quite a few of us to Marxism, including Lionel and me. I think most of the people there were converted to Marxism that summer, and we became fellow travelers.

## Lionel Abel

Harold Rosenberg was a good friend. And he introduced me to Phil Rahv. And Rahv was then a C.P. member. Rosenberg was attracted to Communism and repelled by it, as I was. Rahv was fully Communist, utterly ideological.

I never joined the Communist party but I had a WPA job, in a park, supervising school children. And one of the men I worked with was a Christian American, an utterly American WASP. And to my great surprise, he revealed to me that he was a member of the C.P. I can't remember the occasion, but I remember how struck I was by it. And I thought, here I am, Jewish, and he's the real American, and he's a Communist! And I felt that, in that, there was something I didn't understand that was like a key to some puzzle. The puzzle of the political situation.

## William Phillips

There was a new spirit—the spirit of revolution. Somehow the world was going to be remade and particularly in America. We were completely skeptical that this tiny little group of Communists were going to make a revolution in America. And yet we were swept up to some extent by the spirit of hopefulness, of looking into the future.

*Despite Communism's growing prestige among artists and writers, by the middle of the decade, a small number of intellectuals was growing frustrated with the party's ideological rigidity. Sidney Hook, for one, became a leading left-wing critic of the movement after his disgust at being courted by the party to spy for the Soviet Union.*

*Since the inception of* Partisan Review *under the Communists, Phillips and Rahv had been uncomfortable with the party's attempt to make literature subservient to its own political goals. Communist attacks on Modernist literature as "bourgeois" and the party's heavy-handed attempts to control* Partisan Review *added to their growing disenchantment with the movement. All this was only compounded by a growing concern over the Moscow trials and the purge of the Communist intelligentsia in Russia.*

## William Phillips

They were concerned only with their schematic notions of political organization. And we felt that if radicalism is to have any meaning, any value, to be desirable in any way, to be fulfilling in any way, it had to come together with and represent, in a way, the farthest reaches and the most profound forms of modern consciousness. It couldn't simply be something that ignored these things. And if it ignored these things, then in ways in fact that we couldn't foresee completely, it was bound to distort political and human existence.

I hate to use a word that's become cliché by now but we thought that these writers whom I'm calling Modernists reflected the complexity and the alienation of modern life. There's no point in creating a better world or a new world which the left or the Communists claim to be concerned with if you aren't trying to perpetuate the best values of this world. If you are simply negating what seemed to be the most profound and the most interesting and the most humane values of this world, then what's the point of creating another world?

## Lionel Abel

I remember going to a debate between Jay Lovestone [the former leader of the American Communist party], who had his own organization then, and James Cannon, who was the head of the Trotskyists. And the chairman of the debate was Sidney Hook, who had published *Towards an Understanding of Karl Marx*, which we all read. It was a must, at that time, to people who were interested in politics and Marxism. And I remember Hook said, this is an important date since the leaders of these two groups, the Lovestonite and Trotskyist groups, are willing to face each other in debate.

That debate was something which couldn't have happened in Russia. Yet it concerned Russia more than America! It concerned conditions in Russia more than conditions in America. That debate should have taken place in Moscow or in Leningrad. Here it was in New York!

What Hook emphasized was that whereas the Communist party wouldn't discuss politics with either of these groups, these two groups were willing to exchange opinions and face each other in debate. And that raised a question as to the validity of the Communist movement. Why wouldn't they talk to people who disagreed with them? The fanaticism and obscurantism in the C.P. was highlighted by this event, even though the Lovestonites were still pro-C.P.

*In 1936 the party disbanded the John Reed Clubs, to which* Partisan Review *had been attached, in favor of the broader, Popular Front–inspired League of American Writers. Shortly afterward the publication of* PR *was temporarily suspended for lack of funds.*

*During these months, Rahv and Phillips agonized over whether they should break with the party. Trying to reach a decision, they turned to friends such as Lionel Abel and James Farrell. Farrell, an earlier refugee from the party, had already made his name through the publication of his novel* Studs Lonigan. *His diary from the period records Phllips's and Rahv's anxious attempts to come to terms with their feelings about the Communist movement.*

## The Diary of James Farrell

*August 14, 1936*
Rahv and Phillips are now completely disgusted with the official literary left wing set up. I talked with them today on the prospects of dragging *Partisan Review* out from under the boys, forming an alliance with the freer thinking left-wing groups, giving it a vague Trotskyist orientation instead of its present vague Stalinist orientation and thereby giving the magazine the possibility of functioning freely and with more honesty, and with better contributors.

*October 14, 1936*
Haven't heard from Rahv and Phillips in several days. My understanding was that they were to get in touch with me about doing things, parties etc. to get money for Partisan Review. I wonder—is it fear because my opposition to the party of late has been quite open-voiced.

*Late October/early November 1936*

The other night . . . Felix Morrow said that Lionel Abel had told him this story. Rahv and Phillips were—not so long ago—called up on the carpet by the party, asked about their views, about whether or not they intended bringing over *Partisan Review* to the Trotskyites and the Socialist party, etc., and that they had to make what amounted to a confession of faith.

## William Phillips

I was summoned to the ninth floor by one of the cultural commissars of the Communist party and told that I was talking too loosely and too critically of the Communist party and that I was talking to ordinary members of the Communist party. What this man said to me was, if you want to express these skeptical views, talk to us, the leaders of the Communist party, don't talk to what was called the rank and file of the Communist party. That was the gospel of the ninth floor.

## Lionel Abel

They were planning to break with the C.P., and they'd come to my apartment and discuss it—mainly Philip Rahv. Well, I was urging them to do it, and Phil would come to see me, tell me he would like to break with the C.P. I'd say, that's a wonderful idea. He would then tell me how it was impossible! How he couldn't do it. What he was afraid of. All the catastrophes that would ensue, if he did it. And I never believed he would do it. Finally, he did.

## William Phillips

Breaking with the Communist party is a terribly wrenching process, because it's breaking with a whole way of life, not just breaking with one idea, or one belief, or a set of ideas or beliefs. It meant changing your whole way of life. Changing your friends. All my friends, people I had known for years—some people whom I was responsible for convincing to become Communists—

all of these people stopped talking to me. When I walked down the street and they were walking on the same side of the street, they'd cross the street to avoid me, not to look at me. That was not easy.

And it was not easy to be called names by the Communist party in the *Daily Worker*. I was called an imperialist, a reactionary, the worst things, a snake, a traitor to the left, and so on.

*Phillip's and Rahv's fears of breaking with the party stemmed, in large part, from the enormous cultural influence it wielded. The tremendous success of the party's Popular Front policy had brought a host of literary celebrities within the party's orbit, including Ernest Hemingway, Dorothy Parker, Dashiell Hammett, and Lillian Hellman. In addition to its own press, the party could count on sympathy from other publications, such as* The Nation *and* The New Republic, *and even in the pages of* The New York Times.

## Lionel Abel

Rahv's argument was that nobody would write for *PR*. That they would be blacklisted. That the editors couldn't publish anywhere else. If you wanted to write an article for *The Nation*, or some other periodical, that it would be refused because, don't forget, the Moscow trials had taken place, in '36. And *The New Republic* had gone on record that the Trotskyites were fascists, were in league with Hitler. Malcolm Cowley, who wrote those articles, argued in favor of the Moscow trials' truthfulness. In *The New York Times*, Walter Duranty described the trials as fair and valid. So the connection had been established between Trotskyism and Hitlerism. And that meant that any writer who wanted to publish in *PR* had to think twice about it. What Rahv was afraid of was that no one would support his review. And it's true. Very few people did, at first. You see? The publishing houses were infested with C.P.-ers. The proudest and I think most independent writers in America sought the favor of the C.P. Like Hemingway, Sinclair Lewis.

## Diana Trilling

I don't want to carry it to an ultimate statement, such as it was impossible to publish if you weren't sympathetic to the Communist party. That's not true. You could publish. But you published with difficulty. The doors were not open to you. The doors were open, in all fields of the arts, in all fields of communication, if you were sympathetic to the Stalinists. If you weren't, you had a hard time making your way. You had to find your little crevice through which you could squeeze.

## William Phillips

After we broke it meant spreading the word around circles which were influenced by the Communist party to avoid us—to avoid me, that I was no good. Once or twice I couldn't get a job because of that, because the Communists had sent word that I was not to be hired. I still don't know how we did it. It was a kind of youthfulness and foolishness. Maybe if we were older we couldn't have done it. I noticed that many older people stuck to these worn-out ideas and loyalties for a longer time than they should have. Perhaps they couldn't break so easily.

*Vastly outnumbered by Communists and fellow travelers in the intellectual community, Phillips and Rahv began to look for political allies. Lionel Abel and James Farrell were obvious contributors for the new* Partisan Review, *but they were in need of additional sympathetic voices. They found F. W. Dupee, a literary critic equally attracted to the Modernist movement; Dupee's friend, Dwight Macdonald, an emerging political journalist recently graduated from Yale; the future novelist Mary McCarthy, who would become the theater critic for the new magazine; the independently wealthy painter and art critic George L. K. Morris, who would help support the journal; and aspiring art critics Clement Greenberg and Harold Rosenberg. In the next few years they would publish the first work of a young radical writer from Chicago, Saul Bellow.*

## William Phillips

Shortly after our breaking with the Communists, I had met Fred Dupee, a young writer, who was a Communist and an editor of *The New Masses*. He was a real true believer. He acted as if he was a rank-and-file Communist. He used to distribute the *Daily Worker* on the waterfront to longshoremen in addition to writing and editing *The New Masses*. I met him, I began to talk, and I began to argue with him. I tried to convince him that the Communist party was a fraud, was an evil party, was a fake, was full of lies, and at the end of a number of conversations, I seemed to have convinced him of this.

He said to me one day, "I'd like you to meet a friend of mine who's moving left, but floundering. He seems to be moving in the direction of the Communist party. His name is Dwight Macdonald." He had been a friend of Dupee's at Yale. So he arranged a meeting with Dwight Macdonald, Philip Rahv, and himself at my house. We had lunch. We argued all day long. Arguing with Macdonald wasn't easy. He was not necessarily the best, but he was the greatest arguer in the world—a loud arguer. And he didn't give up easily. And we argued, as I say, all day long.

Rahv and I had him backed against the wall, literally, as we were firing arguments against him. It was not easy to do that to Macdonald. He was a big man and he was aggressive, and he didn't easily back down. But we had him backed against the wall. At the end of that day, Dwight Macdonald was convinced that we were right and that the Communists were no good.

We told him that we'd like to revive *Partisan Review* as an independent magazine. And he said that he'd be glad to join with us and that he had a friend who could finance it. And the friend was George Morris, who was a very good abstract painter and a very good critic of painting—a very good art critic. So we met Morris. And I think, if I remember correctly, Dwight was also a friend of Mary McCarthy's. And he convinced her though maybe she didn't need much convincing. She said that she wanted to join with us. And we decided we were going to put out *Partisan Review* as a new and independent magazine.

## Saul Bellow
## Novelist

I was already converted to Trotskyism. At the University of Chicago we had quite a group of writers and they were very alert to new developments. Philip Rahv came and spent a year at Chicago. His then-wife was an architect and was in one of the local firms and so I used to see quite a lot of Rahv. I was one of a group of students to whom he was very kind. He asked whether we had anything to offer to *Partisan Review* and so I submitted "Two Morning Monologues" and that was that. And very pleased I was, too, that he liked them.

I was so naive I didn't have very advanced views. I was wrapped up in poetry and fiction and took very little interest in literary criticism. The [*Partisan Review* critics] seemed to me to be of two kinds, one the professorial type and the other, the free-wheeling type. Harold Rosenberg was a free-wheeling type, whereas Lionel Trilling was a professorial type. And I didn't take too much interest in the professorial ones and I was mad for Harold Rosenberg. On every subject under the sun he had developed a view. He was highly educated in his own independent way and I simply preferred his company and I would rather read him than read the professors.

*Eking out a living through barely attended jobs courtesy of the writers project of the New Deal's Works Progress Administration, Rahv and Phillips began to publish the new* Partisan Review. *It was now an anti-Stalinist journal dedicated to combining literary Modernism with an independent Marxist politics. Their new editor and art critic, George Morris, put up fifteen hundred dollars to support the magazine through its first two years.*

## Lionel Abel

Neither of them had any idea that they were doing something important. You could have argued with them, for hours, that they were doing something important, and they would have denied it.

In fact, that's what did happen. And by the time they were ready to admit it, the magazine was a complete national success, was nationally the most famous literary magazine in America.

*The young anti-Stalinist radicals at City College saw in* Partisan Review *a larger world. They glimpsed through its pages the possibility of a life devoted to writing and thinking.*

### Irving Kristol

*Partisan Review* played a very important role in my life because it was a left-wing anti-Stalinist magazine, very highbrow. The essays in *Partisan Review* were very hard for a young person of limited education. I used to read those articles five times over trying to make sense out of them. So I didn't just read *Partisan Review*, I studied *Partisan Review*. But it's a very good way to cut your intellectual teeth.

I would read Clement Greenberg's art criticism and try to figure out what it was he was saying, or Mary McCarthy, but of course she was very readable. Phillip Rahv, William Phillips. Lionel Trilling I worshiped. His essays in *Partisan Review* were, for me, an event.

Edmund Wilson, George Orwell were writing for that magazine. Poetry by Auden and Yeats. And so we got a general cultural education of a limited kind, nothing before 1900, but in twentieth-century literature and art, we ended up getting a much better education, I think, than most college students get these days, and it all began out of a political impulse.

### Nathan Glazer

There were these essays that everyone felt they had to read. They weren't essays in a classic sense of graceful and discursive, they were concentrated analysis. They presented us with an ideal. I know my first book reviews had to include in them everything that was relevant, everything about the world.

I've always found it astonishing that educators believe the way to reach people is to discuss where they are. I was not interested in where I was. I was bored to death with where I was. If they were going to talk about life on the Lower East Side, I'd say what are you talking about? You want to talk about life in the shtetl, I didn't care either. We wanted to learn about big things. We wanted to learn about the great movements of history, great movements of ideas, the great novels, poems, music.

## William Phillips

We dreamed of having a magazine that would create a new community of writers and intellectuals, that would pull together whatever independent, gifted people there were. We saw this magazine as the vehicle of Modernism and radicalism via a community. We thought of it partly as a personal organ, but partly as the organ of a new community. So when one talks of the New York intellectuals, one is talking about a community.

*The* PR *critics were, above all, politically engaged intellectuals. There was no better example of this than the exiled Soviet leader Leon Trotsky, who had found refuge in Mexico. Both revolutionary hero and writer, Trotsky had led the Soviet army and also produced a brilliant stream of essays on everything from literature to revolution. Doctrinaire in his Marxist beliefs, Trotsky was unpredictably catholic in his literary views, embracing writers for their talent rather than their politics. In creating the new* Partisan Review, *the editors reached out to him, sending him a letter in July 1937.*

> Dear Mr. Trotsky,
> A group of writers in New York City are reviving the *Partisan Review*. We are going to publish it monthly as an independent Marxist journal. The emphasis will be on literature, philosophy, culture in general, rather than on economics or politics.
> We are eager to have you contribute to our pages. . . .

## William Phillips

Trotsky was a major intellectual figure in a way Stalin wasn't. He was a major intellectual figure, equivalent to Lenin, and in some ways more of an intellectual than Lenin was, more of a literary critic than Lenin was. But also, Trotsky had the germ of a criticism of the Soviet Union from a radical point of view. And to that extent, we learned something from Trotsky, although we didn't accept a number of things of his. He was an imposing figure. And he gave us the vocabulary to criticize the Soviet Union without a right-wing point of view.

## Lionel Abel

Well, you know, the Communists, the Stalinists—we called them Stalinists, at that time—boasted that they had control of 6 percent of the world's surface. I think the Soviet Union, at that time, covered 6 percent of the land surface of the globe. That was in imitation of the British, who were proud of the fact they had an empire on which the sun never set. They said, well, we have 6 percent of the land surface of the Earth. The Trotskyites said, in Trotsky we have 6 percent of the world's political intelligence! And, of course, this was appealing to intellectuals, to be connected with a powerful grasp of the political situation.

He was an excellent writer. He had a literary verve, which was unmistakable. He was a great journalist. And behind his journalism was a great career as commander of the Red Army, the designer of the October Revolution. The coup d'etat was Trotsky's work. And the intellectual power of his criticism of the Stalin regime, most of which has been accepted, nowadays, as justified, was that he was right.  But we didn't know he was right. We knew he was *interesting*. And, in a way, if you lived in the Village, what was interesting was right! Certainly, the uninteresting was wrong! Now, I'm not willing to altogether give that up, even today.

*In* Partisan Review *and its coterie of intellectuals, Trotsky hoped to find new adherents for the small Fourth International revolutionary movement he had founded in exile as a base for his political revival. (In breaking away from the Socialist Second International in 1915 over what stance to take toward World War I, Lenin had created the Third or Communist International movement. Marx himself had helped convene the First International years earlier.)*

*Dwight Macdonald did become a follower, but Rahv and Phillips, after their bruising experience with the Communist party, were determined to keep their magazine independent.*

### William Phillips

Trotsky wanted us to become Trotskyites, join with him. He wanted us to accept not only his leadership, but most, if not all of his ideas—especially his ideas about politics, and about his political organization, about the Soviet Union, about literature, and so on. And we weren't ready to do that. I don't know whether you have a letter of Trotsky where he criticized us for not going along with him. He said we weren't true revolutionaries. Which was true. We weren't true revolutionaries anymore—assuming that one knew what a true revolutionary was anyway.

> *January 20, 1938*
> Dear Mr. Macdonald,
> I shall speak with you very frankly inasmuch as reservations or insincere half-praises would signify a lack of respect for you and your undertaking.
> It is my general impression that the editors of *Partisan Review* are capable, educated, and intelligent people but they have nothing to say. They seek themes which are incapable of hurting anyone but which likewise are incapable of giving anybody a thing. I have never seen or heard of a group with such a mood gaining success, i.e., winning influence and leaving some sort of trace in the history of thought.

Note that I am not at all touching upon the content of your ideas (perhaps because I cannot discern them in your magazine). "Independence" and "freedom" are two empty notions. But I am ready to grant that "independence" and "freedom" as you understand them represent some kind of actual cultural value. Excellent! But then it is necessary to defend them with sword, or at least with whip, in hand. Every new artistic or literary tendency (naturalism, symbolism, futurism, cubism, expressionism, and so forth and so on) has begun with a "scandal," breaking the old respected crockery, bruising many established authorities. This flowed not at all solely from publicity seeking (although there was no lack of this). No these people—artists, as well as literary critics—had something to say. They had friends, they had enemies, they fought, and exactly through this they demonstrated their right to exist.

So far as your publication is concerned, it wishes, in the main instance, apparently to demonstrate its respectability. You defend yourselves from the Stalinists like well-behaved young ladies who street rowdies insult. "Why are we attacked?" you complain, "we want only one thing: to live and let others live." Such a policy cannot gain success.

Leon Trotsky

## William Phillips

Trotsky turned viciously against Dwight Macdonald. Macdonald had been drawn to Trotsky, and then critical of Trotsky and Trotsky responded with his kind of vitriolic rhetoric. He said everybody has a democratic right to be stupid, but Dwight Macdonald abuses the privilege! The sequel to that story is that some people came around raising funds for Trotsky and they rang Dwight Macdonald's doorbell and asked him to contribute to Trotsky. Macdonald said, "Tell Trotsky to go fuck himself!"

*A center of bohemian cultural life since the turn of the century, the Village attracted young would-be writers and intellectuals from across the country. Saul Bellow, who had grown up in Chicago, would often visit friends in New York City and stay in the Village. Lionel Abel, a native of Joplin, Missouri, had recently moved to the Village after graduating from the University of North Carolina.*

## Lionel Abel

The aim of most of my college friends was to come to New York. Most of them wanted to write. And the Village was a refuge from small town life for young Americans. So it was very attractive to me. In a way, everybody came to escape small town life. Bourgeois society. Financial problems. One could live in the Village very inexpensively.

The Village, at that time, was not a place *for* promiscuity. It was a place of refuge from the promiscuity of social life in the sense that you could see the kind of people whom you liked to see, and not businessmen. You see it has a reputation that sexual promiscuity was possible in the Village. Well, that's true, too. But it was also *the avoidance* of other kinds of promiscuity that was appealing.

## William Phillips

Our life was bounded by the boundaries of the Village. The Village was where writers lived. It was not just the headquarters, the region of the Communist party. It was the region of bohemia.

We lived in tiny apartments, the rent was negligible. Some people lived in what were called "cold water flats." There was hot water, but there was no heat as I recall. And the bathtub in those apartments was usually in the kitchen. They were very cheap. They may have cost fifteen dollars a month, or twenty dollars a month. But I paid—I was married then—about thirty-five to forty dollars a month for rent. A vast sum, obviously. Which we could barely afford.

## Saul Bellow

My friend Isaac Rosenfeld got a scholarship to NYU—I think it was to study with Sidney Hook. I used to go quite often from Chicago to see him by bus. It was a nice unbroken trip of thirty-six hours, except that it stopped every two hours at comfort stations. He was in the Village on Barrow Street near Christopher Street. It was marvelously romantic and we were just a short ferry ride from Hoboken—a nickel ferry ride—and we would go to eat clams and drink beer. I was mad for the city and I used to count the days till I could make the journey myself and go to live in New York.

## Lionel Abel

There were people like e. e. cummings, whom you used to see walking around Washington Square Park. I got to know him slightly, much later. Maxwell Bodenheim [the Modernist poet and noted bohemian] was a familiar figure. And there were any number of sculptors and painters.

You rubbed shoulders with actors, playwrights, painters, people interested in ideas, generally. And then there were poetry readings in the Village, at which poets of some national importance came and read from their work. And there were always discussions. And there were girls from Ohio and Seattle and Washington and Oregon, who had found life impossible in their communities, and who were vivacious and interested in people, who were interested in ideas. So I think the conversation in the Village was much better than any place else, except in the halls of learning.

## William Phillips

You must remember we had no money. This was shortly after the worst part of the Depression. So we hung out in cafeterias where we'd have a cup of coffee, maybe a piece of cake, sat there for hours talking, arguing, settling the affairs of the world. We were a very argumentative bunch. And very presumptuous when you stop to think of it.

## Lionel Abel

At Romany Marie's Tavern, which was on Fourth Street, Bertrand Russell came, occasionally (I think Will Durant brought him), and other people who were celebrated: There was an explorer who had been to the North Pole and there is where I first saw Arshile Gorky, as a young painter. He must have been twenty-nine or thirty. He used to come there. Now, when I was hungry, Romany Marie would serve me dinner. A wonderful dinner! On the house! There was no other place in the city like that. Certainly not uptown. She felt that she had some obligation to people who visited her tavern. So the Village was like a village. It combined the intimacy of village life with sophistication.

*In August 1939, the era of the Popular Front abruptly came to an end when Stalin secretly signed a nonaggression pact with Adolf Hitler. Overnight American Communists abandoned their alliance with Roosevelt, confirming the anti-Stalinist left in its belief that the party was being manipulated to suit Stalin's own needs.*

## Irving Howe

I can remember the most terrible few days of my life, intellectually speaking, came after the Hitler-Stalin Pact in 1939. And my friends and I walked around and we felt in one sense we had been confirmed since Trotsky had predicted a Hitler-Stalin pact, but we also felt that we were at a terrible historical point. That the two main totalitarian dictators, the two monsters, had come together, that a war was certain to follow very soon.

*A week after the signing of the pact, Germany invaded Poland and the Second World War began. Within a year, Soviet armies had occupied Lithuania, Latvia, Estonia, Finland, and the eastern portion of Poland.*

*Two years later, in June 1941, Hitler attacked the Soviet Union and Stalin proclaimed the Popular Front once again. That December America entered the war, whereupon a fight broke out among the editors of Parti-*

san Review *for editorial control of the magazine. Clement Greenberg and Dwight Macdonald, in their "Ten Theses Against the War," proclaimed their revolutionary stance against the imperialist war, declaring that "all support of whatever kind must be withheld from Churchill and Roosevelt." Rahv and Phillips countered with their "Ten Theses and Eight Errors," giving support to the fight against Hitler, a primary goal, they believed, even for radicals. Greenberg and Macdonald soon left the magazine.*

### Diana Trilling

If you look at some of *Partisan Review*'s political editorials in the early years before the United States was in the war, between 1937 and our entrance in the war in 1941, it is not only stupid, it is feebleminded. Those editorials are incredible! I don't know how any intellectual can read them without wanting to bury his head in shame. This is the best one could produce? It is not to be believed. The identification of Roosevelt with Hitler; Roosevelt and Churchill were being identified with Hitler.

### William Phillips

We were a mixture of sophistication and naivete. We were so naive in many matters. Reading Marx, Lenin, Bukharin. There was a kind of radical exhilaration going on all around us. Here we were, still kids more or less. Slightly overgrown kids, maybe. But kids. And here we are settling all the affairs of the world. What the future of literature was. What was wrong with Marx, what was wrong with Engels, what was right or wrong with the Soviet Union, what the policy of America should be.

### Saul Bellow

When the Russians invaded Finland the great question was, Could this possibly be an imperialist war? Everyone was waiting for Trotsky to dissociate himself from the USSR, but he remained entirely loyal. He refused to change his mind about the Soviet Union. He kept saying that it was a degenerate worker's state, but a worker's state nonetheless. Trotsky insisted that a worker's state—even a decadent one—could not wage an imperialist war. On grounds of Marxist orthodoxy we were forbidden to think so. So you soon found that you shouldn't be taking any of it seriously because it was silly in so many ways, pleasant ways, not pretentious, not exaggerated, just a little bit on the wild side. It was the defeat of the honest Marxists that came at about that time. You realized you couldn't count on Marxists, even when they were intellectuals in good standing, to make the kind of sense that you wanted to hear.

## Irving Howe

Many of the ideas that we had at the time—ideas of social revolution—seem now half-baked or irrelevant to American conditions. But then you must remember that the situation in the thirties was so utterly different from what it is today, there really was a feeling of apocalypse, that I think is the essential thing. There was the feeling that we were living at the end of the world, and in a way, we were.

## Phillip Selznick

It's really embarrassing to recall these things sometimes but there were three things that we felt were important: Love, and Science, and the Movement. And that went on—charming in its way, I suppose—for at least a couple of years. The draft was looming. One thing that sticks in my mind from the Trotskyist press is a cartoon, a picture of Hitler—I think it was late, 1939 or '40—with the line underneath, "The German Workers Will Shut Him Up." I always remember that as such folly, a visual example of folly—of those people—of us.

*Marxism had taught the anti-Stalinists of* Partisan Review *and City College that only a worldwide revolution by workers could destroy Hitler.*

*American capitalism was the enemy every bit as much as Hitler. But with the coming of the war, they had finally been forced to confront their radical beliefs.*

### Daniel Bell

America went to war against Hitler. Do you say, I'm anti-American? I don't like this country? It's a dreadful country? Then how do you explain it went to war against Hitler? Was it only to save capitalism? Nonsense.

Clearly, the country showed itself in terms of its older traditions. And in terms of its sense of being a nation committed to certain ideals. So, how could you ignore the most obvious fact of one's life? That there was a war against fascism. And this country had stood for it.

# 5. The Newness of Ideas

IT WAS WONDERFUL TO BE A YOUNG INTELLECTUAL IN NEW YORK IN THE
LATE 1940S AND EARLY 1950S. IT WAS INTOXICATING, EXHILARATING.
THERE WERE SO MANY SMART PEOPLE AROUND, AND YOU KNEW MANY
OF THEM. YOU COULD EVEN, ON OCCASION, WRITE SOMETHING THAT
THEY WOULD READ, AND FOR A YOUNG PERSON, THIS WAS HEAVEN.

—*Irving Kristol*

*America's entry into World War II in December 1941 proved a decisive
moment in the lives of the New York intellectuals. Revolutionary rhetoric
and Marxist theory ultimately bowed to the reality of a global conflict
against Nazi Germany, an enemy both fascist and anti-Semitic. Irving
Howe and Irving Kristol spent the war years in the army, Howe in Alaska
and Kristol in southern France. Glazer remained a student at City College while Bell, excused from the draft for poor eyesight, became the managing editor of the socialist magazine* The New Leader. *With the war's
end each emerged into an America thrust out of the Depression, whose
suddenly booming economy offered opportunities even for penniless writers
like themselves.*

## Irving Kristol

After the war, suddenly things seemed possible that had been
utterly impossible. I came out of the army convinced that the
economy was going to collapse. Instead we took off on this wonderful boom and people of my generation, if they wanted to,
could buy a home, could own a car. You must understand, no one
I ever knew owned a car, or owned a home. And started having
families, didn't have to live with in-laws. After ten years of Depression and four years of war, to be able to buy a house and have

children and buy a car—that was fantastic. Jobs started turning up which seemed unthinkable eight years earlier and so the years between 1945 and 1953 were absolutely golden years.

When I married I was not quite twenty-two. I'd lived in Brooklyn all of my life, as had my wife. For me, coming to Manhattan, which was the city, was liberation. We always referred to Manhattan as "the city." We're going to the city. That's where the action was. That's where a lot of people were. Brooklyn was rather dull—pleasant, but dull—and while I never had any firm ambitions in those days, I had one: to get out of Brooklyn. We knew we were going to live in Manhattan and we did. It was the only place for young people to live.

I never liked Greenwich Village because I don't like bohemianism, never wanted to live among bohemians. I knew bohemians, but even then I was very bourgeois. The Upper West Side was the bourgeois place in New York you could afford. You could get a large apartment on Riverside Drive or West End Avenue. We knew we were going to have children and it seemed like a good place to live. There were lots of people that we knew. Alfred Kazin lived on the next block on West End Avenue. We ended up living in the same apartment house with Irving Howe and his wife.

## Nathan Glazer

To be in Manhattan was significant. That's where the action was, and that's where your friends would be gathering. There was a different ethos. The Bronx and Brooklyn was where your parents lived. Manhattan was where you lived if you were involved in intellectual activity.

I got married young, as so many of us did, and then we got an apartment in Rego Park, Queens, actually close to Manhattan by contemporary standards but it felt very far out. We would meet people who were living in Greenwich Village and in Manhattan, and whenever we did, we ended up taking the subway back to Queens so we said, "We have to move to Manhattan," and if you had to move to Manhattan, you had two alternatives. One was Greenwich Village, and the other was the Upper West Side. Gramercy Park and the Upper East Side we couldn't afford, so, we moved to the West Side, to 106th Street.

## Daniel Bell

During the war years, I was managing editor of *The New Leader*. Writers would come there. Particularly after we went to press, we kept Friday as an open day. So I remember Sidney Hook coming in, or Max Eastman, or the black writer Claude McKay, who had been an editor with Max Eastman's *Liberator*. Saul Levitas was the publisher of *The New Leader*, and he had a great circle of friends. Everybody would drop in. There was a great sense of intellectual exchange. It had a great vivacity.

I married in 1943, and then a year later my wife became pregnant. We had a one-room apartment on Tenth Street near University Place. And even though we were just one block from Second Avenue, we were really miles away, in a different world. We were oriented more towards University Place and the Village. We moved out of the Lower East Side, we moved into the Village. For social purposes, we would go west, down to the Village, the St. Remo Bar, and the jazz bars. We'd go to Nick's and to Julius's. Those were our hangouts. We all gravitated westward. That was the basic theme. Go west, young man!

At that time, there was a radio station called WEVD—W. Eugene Victor Debs—and I had a radio program. I did a news commentary once a week, about fifteen minutes. So I'd go down to the studio of WEVD, and do that.

I was constantly working, constantly on the go, constantly involved with writing, meeting, speaking. I started a first book then. I did an article, and John Chamberlain, who at that time was a book reviewer for *The New York Times*, was very taken with it, and he introduced me to John Day. I had a contract for a book, it was called then *The Monopoly State*, dealing with the way in which the economy was becoming a war economy. And I would go up to the Forty-Second Street Library, and work there in the evenings and then, having written about 150 pages—which I still have in my basement—I thought, What do I know about this? Who am I kidding? This is silly. I took books seriously. So I abandoned it.

## Nathan Glazer

I was looking for a job. I went to Dan Bell, I assume everyone else did, too. I had met him when I was editing our student Zionist newspaper at City College. But Dan seemed to know an awful lot. He knew what was going on. He had antennae out.

Dan told me about Max Horkheimer. He had been hired by the American Jewish Committee to study anti-Semitism, and I already thought of myself as a sociologist. And I went to see him, and I had lunch with him and Leo Lowenthal. I became his reader in American social science.

We were on the same floor as the *Contemporary Jewish Record* of the American Jewish Committee, and I talked with the people there, and they needed an editor, and I moved over.

*In 1945 the American Jewish Committee transformed the* Contempo-*rary Jewish Record into a new magazine called* Commentary. *Its first editor, Elliot Cohen, a southern Jew, was an imposing man of legendary brilliance. Balding, with a high forehead, he was remembered by Diana Trilling in her memoir,* The Beginning of the Journey, *as having the "head of an Assyrian king, aquiline, massive, high domed." Under him,* Commentary *became an important intellectual journal of the postwar years. Nathan Glazer wrote for and edited a section called "The Study of Man," which explored the burgeoning social sciences. Its staff also included Clement Greenberg, the art critic and former editor of* Partisan Review, *and Robert Warshow, an early critic of film and popular culture. It quickly attracted young would-be writers like Irving Kristol, then in England with his wife, Gertrude Himmelfarb, who was studying at Cambridge University.*

## Irving Kristol

While I was in Cambridge, England, I started writing for *The New Leader* and I wrote for *Commentary*. I wrote an article and I wrote two or three book reviews. When we came back to New York I had no prospects and very little money but I very much wanted a job as a writer or an editor. It turned out that *Commentary* was looking for an assistant editor, and I had shown them I could write. I was writing lots of things that interested them, and so they employed me as an assistant editor.

Nat and I of course were very close. We used to play chess during our lunch hours and talk about anything and everything.

## Nathan Glazer

We'd start before lunch and play through lunch and continue after lunch for a few hours. In the course of my life, I've discovered that work keeps on increasing. At *Commentary*, we seemed to have plenty of time for everything.

One of the topics that interested me was social psychology: the studies of anti-Semitism, the studies that Horkheimer and his group were doing at the American Jewish Committee, and similar studies that were being done at the Anti-Defamation League. I wrote an article on Japanese concentration camps, that is, the camps in which we relocated the Japanese, because there were books coming out on that experience. And simultaneously, I was taking courses at Columbia, evening courses or late afternoon courses, and thinking I would be a sociologist. There was a sense of hope in the social sciences then, that they would really give us answers to social problems.

## Irving Kristol

During my first three years at *Commentary*, the writing I did was entirely literary and philosophical. I wrote on Freud, I wrote on Einstein, believe it or not. I wrote reviews of Edmund Wilson, reviews of Robert Penn Warren. I wrote on Jewish theology and what was missing, a very presumptuous article, but still it had a point.

I became the religion editor at *Commentary* since I was the only member of the staff who was really interested in what rabbis thought, and so they'd give me the rabbis' articles to rewrite. You couldn't edit them. They had to be rewritten. But I liked that.

It was a very stimulating place to work. At the time, of course, one didn't realize how stimulating and at the time one didn't realize that Clem Greenberg was a great art critic. I just thought he was an art critic and I didn't realize what I realize now, that Bob Warshow really was an originator in popular criticism, in the criticism of popular culture and the appreciation of popular culture. I just thought he was a wonderful thinker and writer, that's all.

### Nathan Glazer

*Commentary* was an important place. It was one of the few places that paid. In retrospect, it didn't pay that much, two hundred dollars an article, but two hundred dollars for an article in 1945 to '50 or so was much more than you got anywhere else.

People would show up, we'd find a book for them to review. We would talk to them. It was a way of keeping in touch with the New York intellectual world, Jewish aspects of it, political aspects of it, and so on. James Baldwin was sent to us and you'd think of a topic, and you'd say, "How about anti-Semitism in Harlem?" And sure enough, he'd come up with it, and it's one of his important essays.

People would say that every novel was reviewed under the general slogan, "It isn't Tolstoy." And none of them were, of course, and people who wrote novels were rather upset at that.

### Irving Kristol

We had a lot of interesting German refugees writing for us, because most of them were Jewish. They needed a magazine that could help them get their articles written in English. They would write in English, but it was not very good. So *Commentary* spent a lot of time "Englishing" those articles. I just noticed that a book came out on Siegfried Kracauer, the quasi-Marxist film critic. Quite famous, it turns out. He used to write for *Commentary*. But we had to take his articles which were written in English by a German— the distinction in his mind between German and English was not very clear—and we had to "English" them. Sometimes running them right through a typewriter.

Mary McCarthy and Hannah Arendt also began to write for *Commentary*. I was their editor, so to speak, but I dared not change a word! But I was their editor. Hannah Arendt didn't come very often but whenever she entered the room she struck everyone as somebody with a strong personality. Mary McCarthy was girlish, beautiful, and you knew that she was brilliant and capable of being savage in some of her stories, so she was really a bit terrifying.

### Nathan Glazer

I recall in particular Irving Howe's first visit to *Commentary*, when he was trying to start a new life. He had stayed with his radical group longer than most, longer than anyone else we knew, and finally the time had come when he felt he ought to make a real living in the world! That was the way it looked to me, and what could he do? He could write book reviews. So he showed up.

*Irving Howe remained a Marxist far longer than his City College friends, maintaining his allegiance to a group that was evolving from Trotskyism to socialism. But he was inching his way into the intellectual world as a writer and literary critic as well.*

### Irving Howe

I had been partly transformed by my experiences in the army. I spent two years in Alaska. It was like a graduate school for me. During that time I read a good many books. There was nothing else to do up there. I began to develop incipient literary incli- nations, to move away from being just political, and I began to contribute a book review here, a book review there.

On the one hand, I was still involved in the little left-wing group although more and more uncomfortable in it, and at the same time I was involved in this world of New York intellectuals, though not entirely at ease there either. And then that began to change.

I worked for a while as an assistant to Hannah Arendt at Schocken Books, which was then a very distinguished publishing company, and I would meet with her every two weeks presumably to do business but actually to engage in intellectual discussion and that was very stimulating. And one thing led to another. And so my horizons widened.

I began to meet some New York intellectuals, like Lionel Trilling and Harold Rosenberg, Philip Rahv, and most important-ly for me, Meyer Schapiro, who was sort of my idol and guru. I remember going up to the offices of *Partisan Review* and being received by Philip Rahv in a rather gruff, but friendly manner. And he handed me the chance to do a review and that was a big opportunity it seemed and in fact it was.

### Irving Kristol

It was wonderful to be a young intellectual in New York in the late 1940s and early 1950s. It was intoxicating, exhilarating. There were so many smart people around and you knew many of them. You could even, on occasion, write something that they would read, and for a young person, this was heaven.

*Long inspired by* Partisan Review, *the four young men were beginning to write for it, and* Partisan Review *was becoming an important force in American intellectual life. The journal's circle of writers and critics were finding their voices in postwar America.*

*Lionel Trilling was becoming one of the country's preeminent literary critics through work such as* The Liberal Imagination. *His wife, Diana, had begun publishing literary criticism as well. Through their work as crit-ics and professors, Alfred Kazin, F. W. Dupee, Philip Rahv, and William*

*Phillips were securing a foothold in American culture for the Modernist lit-*
*erature they had long admired.*

*Art critics Clement Greenberg, Harold Rosenberg, and Meyer Schapiro*
*had begun to champion the diverse group of artists who would come to be*
*known as the New York Abstract Expressionist painters, making their own*
*names in the process.*

*Dwight Macdonald continued his work as a political essayist, starting*
*his own short-lived but influential journal* politics *and later becoming a con-*
*tributor to* The New Yorker. *Sidney Hook remained the group's unofficial*
*philosopher-in-residence.*

*Through books like* The Company She Keeps, *Mary McCarthy had*
*metamorphosed into a writer of fiction. And future Nobel laureate Saul Bel-*
*low was winning acclaim for his novels* Dangling Man *and* The Adventures of Augie March.

*And now they had been joined by a new generation. Questioning old*
*Marxist political beliefs, they were struggling to understand the world from*
*a new, less certain place.*

## Irving Kristol

The army for me was a very profound education, because I was a
New York kid, a New York Jewish kid. I didn't know anything
about America. And I didn't know anything about most ordinary
people.

I enlisted in Chicago. About half of my original group seems
to have come from Cicero, Illinois, which was Al Capone's home
town, or at least, his criminal base, and they were very tough and
very anti-Semitic. I looked at them and thought, "You know, I
don't think we can create socialism with these people and since
I'm not going to kill all the people—we have to live with them—
I think it would be better to rethink socialism." I realized that to
create a new socialist person, which was our ideal, was probably a
utopian enterprise, that the American working class was not what
socialists thought it was.

At that point the notion of socialism as a political vision to be realized collapsed. And so I became a social democrat and by the 1940s I was a sort of liberal.

*The Protestant theologian and political activist Reinhold Niebuhr (1892–1971) exerted an enduring influence on many in the American liberal community. A former socialist turned Cold War liberal, Niebuhr blended a neo-Augustinian view of man as inherently flawed sinner with a hard-edged political realism, producing a critique of utopian political philosophy that resonated with the disillusioned radicals in New York.*

### Irving Kristol

It didn't matter whether you believed in original sin or not. If you were impressed by Niebuhr you came to the conclusion that utopian politics was foolish. It was against human nature, against the order of the world. If you're against utopian politics you end up being deradicalized. Niebuhr played a very important role in deradicalizing an awful lot of people. He was very important to us in defining the limits of the political. Niebuhr himself was a liberal and a lot of us remained liberals—but chastened liberals, liberals with no grand or great expectations as to what political action could achieve.

### Daniel Bell

I began reading Max Weber as a graduate student at Columbia, reading Dostoevski's *The Possessed*—all of these made clear that the radical absolutist position was going to be not only self-defeating but lead to some horrifying results. It goes back to the theme Irving Kristol and I used to discuss. That utopia was necessary as a standpoint, but to try to realize it on earth involved distortions which were dreadful.

Man is a finite creature. He is limited. Man is homoduplex. He has the capacity for love, and the capacity for hate. So that what you have with Niebuhr is the emphasis on man's finitude. The vocabulary which came into play at that point was the note of limits. You need to have limits.

## William Phillips
### Editor, *Partisan Review*

There was a disillusionment with the Marxist clichés, a shunning
of certain pat left-wing ideas which hadn't been challenged; ideas
which traveled from Marx and Engels down all the way through
Lenin and even through Trotsky.

To be a radical Communist in the thirties meant you didn't
have to think. It wasn't necessary to think. In fact, it was a hin-
drance. All you had to do was to know what the answers were.
After a while, you forgot what the questions were. We were
leaving that behind. We decided to face certain questions hon-
estly.

*In their disillusionment with Marxism, in their desire to face the political
realities before them, the New York intellectuals realized that radicalism
had, in fact, blinded them to America.*

## Nathan Glazer

One of the things that made us distant from America was the fact
that we weren't Democrats or Republicans. That's certainly a way
of distancing yourself from your culture and its politics, if you
don't participate in any practical element of it. That distancing was
beginning to break down under the impact of experience.

I remember the day after the election of 1948, when Harry
Truman won and I had voted for Norman Thomas and I felt
silly about it. And a number of other people I knew felt silly
about it. We liked Norman Thomas but we felt we were a little
unrealistic.

## Daniel Bell

Socialist politics was impossible given the nature of the American
political system. The Socialist party was becoming more and more
futile. The Socialists had said that there was no possibility of
changing the system. They didn't want to take full responsibility

for things. They wanted to be pure, not be compromised. And I think part of the tragedy of socialism was the inability to move out of this box.

Roosevelt had shown one could change the system. We were coming out of the Depression, clearly some answers were possible. The New Deal had created Social Security, labor bargaining, the growth of a trade union movement. A welfare state was emerging. The Democrats were taking over much of the socialist platform, so I moved into the Democratic party.

## Irving Kristol

While Manhattan was not America and still is not America, it brought us in touch with people who knew something about America and knew something about the world, people who had been to Paris, people who had been to Washington, even. The first man I ever met who had actually been to Washington was Arthur Schlesinger, Jr., and he kept telling us, "You know, you're very bright and all that, but you really don't understand American politics. You don't understand what America's like." And he was right. But of course we didn't believe him. We had read all the right books, you see.

## Norman Podhoretz
## Assistant Editor, *Commentary* magazine

A lot of the New York intellectuals were quite provincial, and they knew very little, really, about what went on in America. This was a small group that felt itself alienated, a word that we all came to dislike very much but was common at the time. Like someone who didn't quite belong in this country.

Many in the group had a sense of being a community unto themselves, living by their own rules and standards, by their own passions. So we were cut off, in that sense, from the ruling passions of most Americans, or what some of us imagined to be the ruling passions of most Americans.

*Daniel Bell at age thirteen in 1932 (second row, fifth from right), around the time he joined the Young People's Socialist League.* Courtesy of Daniel Bell.

*The five-year-old Nathan Glazer poses in a suit made for him by his garment-worker father.* Courtesy of Nathan Glazer.

*The young Irving Howe in a posed photograph from the early 1930s.* Courtesy of Nicholas Howe.

*The City College of New York was, in the 1930s and 1940s, an intellectual sparring ground where students debated the burning issues of socialism, communism, democracy, and capitalism. Clockwise from top, four of the student body's leading lights: Irving Kristol (class of 1940) at right in the photo above; Daniel Bell (class of 1939); Irving Howe (class of 1940); and Nathan Glazer (class of 1943), during their years at City College.* Courtesy of Irving Kristol, Daniel Bell, the City College of New York, and Nathan Glazer.

*Irving Kristol, standing at far right, with fellow members of the City College Student Council.*
Courtesy of the City College of New York.

*The editorial board of the "new" Partisan Review, circa 1937. Clockwise from upper left: George L. K. Morris, Philip Rahv, Dwight Macdonald, William Phillips, and F. W. Dupee.* Courtesy of Riverside Films.

*Leon Trotsky, the exiled Soviet revolutionary who became an intellectual model for the students of alcove one and the editors of* Partisan Review. Courtesy of Dwight Macdonald Papers, Manuscripts and Archives, Yale University Library.

*Irving Kristol in the 1940s, when he was assistant editor of* Commentary *magazine.* Courtesy of Irving Kristol.

*Daniel Bell, Irving Kristol, and the Russian historian Peter Viereck in Florence, Italy, in 1955, during their days with the American Committee for Cultural Freedom.* Courtesy of Daniel Bell.

*In the forties and fifties the* Partisan Review *circle kept in close contact with their European counterparts. Counterclockwise from bottom center: essayist Dwight Macdonald; actor Kevin McCarthy; poet John Berryman; novelist Mary McCarthy; Italian literary critic Nicola Chiaromonte; his wife, Miriam; novelist Elizabeth Hardwick; essayist Lionel Abel; and Bowden Broadwater, the husband of Mary McCarthy.* Courtesy of the Vassar College Library.

*By the mid-1950s, academia had finally welcomed the New York intellectuals. Here Irving Howe lectures at the Salzburg Seminar in American Studies in 1958. The Seminar brought over American academics to teach European students each year.* Courtesy of Nicholas and Nina Howe.

*Tom Hayden, the president of Students for a Democratic Society, helped to write the 1962 Port Huron Statement, the defining document of the New Left.* Courtesy of Tom Hayden.

*Nathan Glazer in the mid-1960s, during his days as a professor at the University of California at Berkeley.* Courtesy of Nathan Glazer.

*In 1964, the Free Speech Movement galvanized and divided the Berkeley campus, pitting liberal professors like Nathan Glazer and Seymour Martin Lipset against the increasingly radical students.* Courtesy of The Bancroft Library, University of California.

In the 1970s and 1980s, Irving Kristol moved further to the right, helping to found the movement known as "neoconservatism" and becoming a behind-the-scenes player at the White House during the Reagan years. From left: unidentified man, columnist George Will, Irving Kristol, and former Chrysler chairman Lee Iacocca chat with President Ronald Reagan. Courtesy of Ronald Reagan Library.

*Irving Howe with his daughter Nina in 1991.* Courtesy of Nicholas and Nina Howe.

*Nathan Glazer and Daniel Bell, retired from teaching but still arguing the world, on the steps of Harvard's Widener Library in 1998.* Photo by Nina Davenport; courtesy of the author.

*At once provincial New Yorkers and cosmopolitan intellectuals, the group around* Partisan Review *and* Commentary *was beginning to produce some of its most interesting and wide-ranging work. Clement Greenberg looked at "The Plight of Our Culture: Industrialism and Class Mobility"; Diana Trilling examined "Men, Women and Sex"; Harold Rosenberg wrote "Notes on Fascism and Bohemia"; Alfred Kazin explored the Broadway theater audience in "We Who Sit in Darkness"; Delmore Schwartz wrote "Masterpieces as Cartoons"; Lionel Trilling penned "A Note on Art and Neurosis"; Irving Howe, with B. J. Widdick, discussed how "The U.A.W. Fights Race Prejudice"; Nathan Glazer took on "The 'Alienation' of Modern Man" and the question of "Why Jews Stay Sober"; Irving Kristol questioned "Is Jewish Humor Dead? The Rise and Fall of the Jewish Joke," and explored "What the Nazi Autopsies Show: The Totalitarian Myth and the Nazi Reality"; Daniel Bell examined the changing economy in "The Prospects of American Capitalism" and in "America's Un-Marxist Revolution: Mr Truman Embarks on a Politically Managed Economy." It was all vintage New York intellectual in its scope and breadth as the group took on Marxism as well as psychoanalysis, fascism and existentialism, art, literature, the union movement, capitalism and the growth of the welfare state.*

### Nathan Glazer

One of the characteristics of our group was a notion of its universal competence: culture, politics, or whatever was going on, we shot our mouths off. I know I did. It's a model created by an initial arrogance that if you're a Marxist you can understand anything, and it was a model that even as we gave up our Marxism, we nevertheless stuck with.

### Alfred Kazin
### Literary Critic

The atmosphere at *Partisan Review* was both exciting because of the wealth of their interests, and insular because of the nature of these people themselves. Saul Bellow began by writing so-called monologues for them—short stories—and he once heard one editor say to the other, "Anything interesting come in today?" And the other one said, "No, just some short stories."

They remained, in certain ways, very timorous, despite their advanced tastes in literature and art. Rahv and Phillips and a lot of the Jewish writers who wrote for it seemed to me to be absolutely engulfed in a kind of domestic scene. They were reliving, as it were, the lives of their Russian parents or relatives.

At the same time, *Partisan Review* was really a marvelous magazine then. *Partisan Review* seemed to be, for a long time, the magazine to write for. And I was always very proud and happy to get a piece in.

## Saul Bellow
## Novelist

*PR* published all kinds of wonderful stuff. People like Arthur Koestler and George Orwell, and all of a sudden we were face to face with our European peers, except they weren't exactly our peers, they were our superiors because we were so green and enthusiastic and they were so worldly and European. When you published something in *Partisan Review* it was just as likely to be flanked by Ignazio Silone on one side and George Orwell on the other, and you felt that you had finally found a place for yourself among the leading figures of the century. And that was very exciting. There was an internationalization of the intellectuals in those years.

## Daniel Bell

Most of us came out of ourselves in that the homes which we came out of, even though emotionally very important and emotionally very warm, didn't provide cultural relationships. My mother was not ignorant or unlettered but she was not an intellectual, so basically it was a change from a nonintellectual into a very different world and so you search out eagerly those with whom you could talk and exchange ideas.

## Norman Podhoretz

They were stuck in the sense that there was almost no one else, outside this particular world, who was capable of participating in the kind of discussion that went on in that world, and that was everyone's passion and life blood. You needed to have read a great deal and not just a great deal, but certain kinds of things. You needed to have a certain kind of mind, you needed to be interested in a certain range of issues, and you needed to be articulate. You needed to be brilliant. That was the quality that was most prized. And brilliant meant quick, able to see and make connections that other people hadn't seen and made. Able to win arguments with other very smart people, and everyone was brilliant in that way.

## Diana Trilling
## Literary Critic

I think that we were trying to create our own culture apart from our families and it was very nice to have a family group. This was a sort of substitute family that spoke more or less the same language and it wasn't the language of their own homes. It was a new, educated, much wider-ranging language.

## Irving Kristol

It was a community that consisted of people who thought they were smarter than everybody else. And were smarter than an awful lot of people. Not necessarily as smart as they thought they were. Particularly about politics. It was assumed that it's easy to be smart about politics. That was the great error of the New York intellectuals, who really ended up having some rather bizarre political opinions on subjects about which they knew very little. As I subsequently discovered. But, the fact is, they were very smart people and they were very widely read, they took ideas very seriously. They argued about ideas seriously, and it was exhilarating.

Religion, politics, you name it, and they developed an opinion. And that's the nature of intellectuals. They had lots of opinions on just about everything. Some of the New York intellectuals did teach at the university, but they did not think of themselves primarily as academics.

## William Phillips

Academics are not intellectuals. Academics are people who teach in universities, and do academic work. Some of them are intellectuals, many are not. An intellectual has an independent mind, a generalizing mind, and an original mind. That I think defines an intellectual, those three qualities. And not all academics have them.

One of the characteristics of the New York intellectuals was our obsession with ideas. And ideas meant defending the ideas, promoting the ideas, arguing. Language was at its best and highest point when it was loudest, and when it was used in argument. Then it was at its most refined and sharpest.

We were always arguing with each other, but within certain premises, which made us a community. As I've often said, "You can't argue with a person who doesn't share any of your premises." He's got to share some of your premises; otherwise, you don't know where to begin. You don't know what to say. Nevertheless we were always probing ideas, probing not only our ideas, but other people's ideas. Why we were like that, I don't know. It's been suggested that it's a Jewish trait. It's a New York trait. It's maybe a cosmopolitan trait.

## Irving Kristol

Someone once pointed out if you were writing a review of a book by someone, and wanted to be nasty, you would say he had written an "academic" book. On the other hand, if an academic were writing a review of a book by an intellectual in a more academic journal and he wanted to be nasty, he would say his book is "brilliant," meaning unsound! The gap between academics and intellectuals was a real one.

Most of the people today who seem to be intellectuals are also professors. And that's all right, I'm not criticizing them for that. At least they don't have to rely on their wives being schoolteachers to be able to pay the bills. But the fact remains that it's different. People are scattered all over the country at different universities. You don't get a community of intellectuals.

## Norman Podhoretz

These people, for me, represented the height of intellectual excitement. They seemed to be, what I guess today you'd call the cutting edge of all ideas in every conceivable area. That was one of the main characteristics of the New York intellectuals: the synoptic mind. These were people who, although some of them were specialists in a given field, specialized in relating ideas to one another, past and present, putting everything in context.

In particular, those who were mainly interested in literature read texts not only closely—that was the heyday of the new criticism—but they also went beyond that and tried to relate given books and poems to the political, cultural, spiritual conditions out of which these works emerged. This was very heady stuff for anyone who had a taste for intellectual adventure.

I think there were very few groups that had the sort of intensity of interaction that the New York intellectuals experienced, and I guess the intensity was partly a product, well, of simple passion. I mean these were people who really cared about ideas, for whom ideas were, if not literally a matter of life and death, almost at least symbolically so and mattered more than almost anything else, in many cases more than personal relations. More than making a living.

## Nathan Glazer

I think one aspect of our intensity was the newness of ideas for us. Nothing was obvious. It wasn't as if we were working over once again the relationship between Nietzsche and Schopenhauer. We'd never heard of Nietzsche, we'd never heard of Schopenhauer. So it was all first hand. Everything was fresh and new. Whatever it was, it was the beginning. And I don't think that's possible if you've had a good education and come from a cultured home.

## Alfred Kazin

You had a feeling among these people that they were inflamed, they were so passionate about things. But, most of all, they were so polemical-minded. The atmosphere was so polemical and so bitterly incestuous that when William Phillips's wife, Edna, died, the thing that everybody said about her at her funeral was that she was the only one who never criticized anybody. You knew when you entered the office, or when you spoke to Rahv and Phillips, that you had to keep your wits about you. You also had to make sure that you were attacking something or somebody.

*The social life of the New York intellectuals in the forties and fifties can be traced to the offices of magazines like* Partisan Review *and* Commentary *where many worked and wrote and many others visited looking for an assignment and some conversation. At night the arguments and the nonstop talk were sometimes boozily reincarnated in what Victor Navasky described as a kind of unofficial "floating Saturday night party."*

## Daniel Bell

One very crucial thing that lubricates parties: gossip, cultural gossip. About who's writing what, who's doing what, who's publishing what. The function of parties is cultural gossip. Many of us had developed friendships and contacts with people in Europe. People traveled so that if people came from France, came from England you gave a party for them, and when you went to France or England, they gave a party for you so a party wasn't simply a party. In that sense, it was an occasion.

## Lionel Abel
### Literary Critic

The painter Marc Chagall, who somewhat resembled Meyer Schapiro, was invited and would come. So you could see the two of them together at a *PR* party. Ignazio Silone, when he was in America, Jean Paul Sartre.

## Saul Bellow

I was wild with happiness to be invited to those parties. There was always something special going on and there were people I simply enjoyed being in the presence of, like [the poet] Delmore Schwartz or [the philosopher] William Barrett, or Phillip Rahv or Dwight Macdonald. And Dwight Macdonald's own place—I think it was on East Tenth Street—was always open and you could drop in and leave when you had had enough. But he welcomed everybody. And you met all kind of oddities there, strange people.

## Helen Frankenthaler
### Artist

I had first become aware of the intellectual world when I was still a student in the mid-forties at Bennington. So I was geared for New York, but I knew nothing about it. As a person always interested in bantering and ideas, this world was very exciting to me, if not rather glamorous. It was Clement Greenberg that introduced me to that. He straddled both the intellectual and the art worlds. And I was so impressed and heart-pounding at the idea of meeting these people that had been heroes or enigmas to me, to see the Trillings, to see Saul Bellow, to see Jackson Pollock.

## Irving Kristol

My major memory of a dinner party is one of William Phillips's. I got a plate of food, and there was a couch, and so I walked over and sat down in the middle of the couch, not knowing who was going to join me, and not really much caring. Well, what happened was, Mary MacCarthy sat down at one side of me, Hannah Arendt sat down on the other side of me, and then Diana Trilling pulled up a chair and sat facing me. And I was a prisoner, I couldn't get out. And they then had a long hour-and-a-half discussion on Freud, in which they were all disagreeing. I don't remember what the dispute was. All I know is I sat there quiet and terror-stricken. And my wife was across the room giggling endlessly.

## Alfred Kazin

They were all Critics with a capital C and they were critics of everything, especially of each other. I always felt when I went to a *Partisan Review* party at Rahv's house that if I went to the bath-room for a moment, they would start attacking me as a matter of course. There's that old joke about Otto Kahn, the German Jewish banker. The joke is Otto Kahn is a Jewish gentleman who becomes a "kike" the minute he leaves the room.

## Diana Trilling

These people didn't know how to behave. Intellectuals knew how to think but they didn't know how to behave! Those parties were absolutely horrible if you weren't on the make, sexually. Then you had no right to be there. You really shouldn't have been there. Especially if you weren't known. Those were the two things: If you weren't a known person, if you weren't a name, then the only way as a woman that you could be justified in being there was to be somebody for a sexual conquest. And if you were neither a name nor sexually available, you should have stayed home, because it was just a misery. Unless a man in the intellectual community was bent on sexual conquest, he was never interested in women. He wanted to be with the men. They always wanted to huddle in a corner to talk.

The wife of William Phillips, Edna Phillips, and the wife of Philip Rahv, Nathalie Rahv, both told me after I got to be friends with them in later years that they had had to take several stiff drinks before every one of those parties in order to get through them, they were so miserable.

I didn't start to write until the forties, and once I was a writer, I was better off, but even then I was still a woman, unfortunately, and I mean unfortunately in their view and not in mine. They were really horrible. Once established as writers, women were treated well intellectually. Professionally they were treated well, indeed. But they were not treated all that well socially.

### Helen Frankenthaler

I remember the first time I met Diana Trilling, my heart was pounding, I mean, this was a big event, it was at William and Edna's, and I think she probably felt, "Oh, this young whippersnapper tag-a-long." I was still half in bobby socks and saddle shoes. I was twenty-one or so. She didn't bother me, or bother with me, that is.

It seemed in those days that there was always an issue and there was a lot arguing and complaining, but in a very healthy and productive way—there was a community. Which doesn't mean that people didn't argue and never want to speak to each other again, too. But, I think it helped shape my future. To argue, see, and hear things for the first time was thrilling. Overthrilling in a way.

### Nathan Glazer

In those days, I think I was less argumentative and less assertive, than, let us say, the most argumentative and assertive ones. Maybe another context brought on those qualities, but I was a junior member, and I felt it.

### Helen Frankenthaler

There was a different kind of ambition towards money, fame, and power. I think the serious world of productive argument and enlightenment and creativity is not now what it was then.

### Diana Trilling

I can remember that I had lunch in the fifties with the editor of one of the very popular women's magazines, like *Glamour*, and I remember this editor saying to me that in recent years every editor of every popular magazine—every large-circulation magazine—had had to decide which way to go to increase circulation. Whether to become more popular or—and these were her exact words—to raid *Partisan Review*. And she said magazines that made the choice to become more popular had lost circulation. And the magazines that had raided *Partisan Review* had become more popular, had increased their circulations.

I think it was an absolutely critical revelation of something that had happened in the culture, and that is a homogenization of the culture so that people who wrote for the popular magazines, let's say anything from *Good Housekeeping* to *Esquire*, could now call on the most serious writers and they were willing to write for those magazines and they had never been able to do this before. I was unique as somebody who wrote for the popular press and *Partisan Review*. Absolutely nobody else but me in the forties, but by the late fifties things had changed.

### Irving Kristol

At that time already, the *Partisan Review* community had begun to break up. More and more people were getting academic jobs, there were political disagreements. Dwight Macdonald went off to write for *The New Yorker*. Mary McCarthy began to write for *The New Yorker*. The highbrow intellectuals began to be accepted by what used to be called middlebrow magazines.

I must tell you, if you go back to *Partisan Review*, in the early forties, the worst thing Mary McCarthy could say of any novelist or short story writer was that he or she appeared in *The New Yorker*. Now *The New Yorker* did not change that much, although it did go upscale a bit, as they say. But the attitudes changed among the intellectuals of *Partisan Review*. It turned out that they didn't want in, so long as they couldn't get in. But once they could get in, it turned out they didn't mind getting in.

# 6. Darkness Descending

THE FREE PEOPLES OF THE WORLD LOOK TO US FOR SUPPORT IN
MAINTAINING THEIR FREEDOM. IF WE FALTER IN OUR LEADERSHIP,
WE MAY ENDANGER THE PEACE OF THE WORLD, AND WE SHALL
SURELY ENDANGER THE WELFARE OF THIS NATION.

*—President Harry S. Truman, addressing Congress, 1948*


CONGRESSMAN: ARE YOU A MEMBER OF THE COMMUNIST PARTY?

HOWARD FAST, AUTHOR: I MUST REFUSE TO ANSWER THAT QUES-
TION, BASING MY REFUSAL UPON THE PRIVILEGE GRANTED TO ME
IN THE FIFTH AMENDMENT.

*—Testimony before the House Committee*
*on Un-American Activities*

*In the postwar years, Bell, Kristol, Glazer, and Howe were stirred into
a greater consciousness of their Jewish identity by a series of overlap-
ping personal and political experiences. The Nazi genocide against
Europe's Jews, reports of which had begun leaking out during the war,
combined with their own deradicalization, forced them to confront more
openly the meaning of their own Jewishness. The creation of the state
of Israel in 1948 and the persecution of Jews under Stalin also played
a critical role in this growing self-awareness. Though they would never
become religiously observant, each of them found ways to express their
Jewish identity.*

*Irving Howe became deeply involved in a revival of Yiddish literature
after the war. He would go on to coedit five anthologies of translations of
classic texts and was instrumental in the discovery for an English-speaking*

*readership of the contemporary Yiddish writer Isaac Bashevis Singer. Kris-*
*tol delved into Jewish theology and became* Commentary's *religion edi-*
*tor. Glazer, a radical Zionist before the war, wrote on prejudice and anti-*
*Semitism as the editor of* Commentary's *"Study of Man" column. His*
*first book,* American Judaism, *examined the sociology of religious obser-*
*vance. During the war, Bell became actively involved in the plight of the*
*radical Jewish Bund, advocating the acceptance of Jewish refugees by other*
*nations.*

## Daniel Bell

The Warsaw ghetto uprising in '43 became a great, great shock.
Many of us were identified with the Jewish Bund. Shmuel Ziggelboim had been sent out by the ghetto to alert the authorities
about what was going on. When there was no response, he committed suicide. Alfred Kazin wrote a beautiful piece in *The New
Republic* about the death of Ziggelboim. The leaders of the Warsaw
ghetto had been smashed.

I was running *The New Leader* and we began to be bothered
by the fact that Jewish refugees were being turned away, both by
Britain and by the United States. One ship had gone to Cuba and
been turned back to Europe and the people had been picked up
and killed. We were very much aware of what was happening to
the Jews of Europe and tried to get an expansion of the refugees
into England, into the United States.

## Irving Kristol

I encountered the Holocaust in Europe; it moved me to get more
seriously interested in Jewish things, turned me toward greater
Jewish self-identification. All of us had come from very Jewish
households, but never thought of ourselves as being particularly
Jewish. But that changed after the war.

I saw a lot of the DP camps—the Displaced Persons camps—
when I was stationed in Marseilles after the war. In the neighbor-

ing port of La Ciotat there was a whole organized exodus of Jews to Israel—all illegal—and so I met those people and chatted with them and brought them food and cigarettes. In fact, the first thing I wrote for *Commentary* when I came out of the army was a two- or three-page short story based on an encounter with one of those people called "Adam and I."

## Nathan Glazer

I can date my responses to the Holocaust from a number of key articles that appeared in *Commentary*. One was one of the earliest direct memoirs of the Warsaw uprising by Ziviah Lubetkin in about '45 or '46. And I remember going to a very early documentary movie about the Holocaust. I was deeply affected without knowing what the proper reaction was. I was trying to make sense of it.

I remember a comment of Irving Kristol's, which stayed with me over the years. He said that the Holocaust will have less effect on the history of man, the human spirit, than the death of three hundred Spartans at Thermopylae because we can't give it a meaning. We know what the meaning of Thermopylae is—heroism. But what is the meaning of the Holocaust? It was something one struggled with.

Around that time, Ernst Simon, who had been a collaborator of Martin Buber's, asked his friend Leo Lowenthal how he could connect with young Jewish intellectuals. Because of my Zionist connections he came to me and asked to meet with some of my friends. He told us of the revival of Jewish interests among intellectuals in Germany in the twenties and offered an opportunity for us to start a study group and we accepted it. It went on for a couple of years. It made none of us practicing Jews. But it played a role, along with the Holocaust, in taking the Jewish identity which had been so suppressed, so ignored and helped reestablish it as part of one's general identity.

## Daniel Bell

With Simon we decided to read the *Mishneh Torah* of Maimonides, but eventually he had to go back to Jerusalem so he
introduced us to a man named Jacob Taubes.

The study group included Irving Kristol, myself, Nathan Glazer, Milton Himmelfarb, later Arthur Cohen. With our wives, we
met every Sunday night for dinner and then sat around the table
reading the *Mishneh Torah*, a line-by-line analysis, and this was a
way of exploring the nature of Jewish thought. We were learning
some of the key books of the tradition and understanding what
Judaism was all about. Irving, particularly, had very strong religious
interests.

## Irving Kristol

It was fascinating to read it closely and see what Maimonides was
up to. Taubes was a brilliant teacher. I didn't know exactly what to
do with my Jewishness. I did want to understand the religious
dimension. I was interested in the religious aspect of being Jewish
in an intellectual way so I started reading.

At the same time we did want to retain the universality of
ideas. And one of the things I didn't like about Jewish intellectual
life was how parochial it was, and how parochial our communal
institutions were. There was very little to read at the time and the
only Jewish thinkers who, in my opinion, were terribly important
in life—Martin Buber, Franz Rosenzweig—had yet to be translat-
ed into English. There wasn't very much that I found interesting.
The intellectual level of German Jewry in the 1920s—*even in the
thirties*—was so much higher than that of American Jewry. So I
was stumbling along.

## Nathan Glazer

We were more aware of, and accepting, and involved in Jewish
issues than the first generation of New York intellectuals. I felt that
it was odd that most of the *PR* group was so divorced from this

whole realm. It may have been a response to the nature of the times.

Even though we had grown up in a period of anti-Semitism, by the forties the whole notion of assimilation and adaptation was different from what it had been in the thirties. Maybe it was Hitler, and a number of factors that changed the cultural milieu. In the earlier generation one sees a direct pushing away of Jewishness and in the later generation, one lived with it even though it formed variable parts of one's consciousness.

In about '54 or '55, Daniel Boorstin asked me to give lectures that became my book, *American Judaism*. The assignment led to a serious period of research and thinking about the role of Jews in America—what will happen to them, what is their future. And the rise of the state of Israel put on the agenda permanently the question of international Jewish politics and the question of the unique vulnerability of the Jewish people.

*In the past, none of the four men had advocated the establishment of a Jewish homeland.* Commentary *and its parent organization, the American Jewish Committee, were both ambivalent about the creation of a Jewish state. Among many Jews there was a desire to focus on the Jewish community in America mixed with a concern that Jewish self-interest would be perceived as conflicting with the community's loyalty to the United States. Bell, Glazer, Kristol, and Howe, under the influence of Marxist political universalism, had never focused on the question of purely Jewish statehood. Even Nathan Glazer, as a radical Zionist at City College, believed that any new state in Palestine should represent the binational interests of Arabs and Jews alike. The founding of the State of Israel in 1948 soon changed all this.*

### Nathan Glazer

Even though we were Zionists, in Avukah we were against the Jewish state and for binationalism. In retrospect it was politically impossible. Hannah Arendt was writing long articles against the Jewish state and *Commentary* was publishing some of them.

I was connected to David Riesman who was connected to Erich Fromm who knew Albert Einstein and there was a coming together of a group of people from different backgrounds and very different perspectives (Riesman had an assimilationist position whereas Fromm and Einstein had a universalist position), all of whom were skeptical, who felt that the establishment of the Jewish state simply as a Jewish state would be a problem.

After Israel became a state, I became fully committed—that the Jewish state must survive. I saw it as being surrounded by danger.

### Irving Kristol

Like all socialists in those days I was a universalist. Socialists in those days were not Zionists. *The Forward* was not a pro-Zionist paper. It was anti–Zionist. My deradicalization was in part a movement toward Zionism.

With the DP camps I realized that these people needed a place of refuge. And with the Holocaust, I felt that God owed us something and the state of Israel was what he gave us.

### Daniel Bell

I had always identified with the Bund. Zionism felt like an alien notion. What is Israel? What is Palestine? It made no sense. Our problems were living where we were. And dealing with the class struggle or class problems of where we live.

When I was teaching in Salzburg in '53 there were still DP camps. And I realized the only place these people could go was Israel. So you realized there was a certain point at which having a place like that was a basis of survival. We knew the history of the Jews—the history of survival was that of the remnant. So here's a place of survival. Particularly since the Bund had almost been wiped out. And as the notion that we had to be completely oriented to our own country began to change, so Israel began to loom larger in our minds.

*In the years after the war, revelations from Stalin's Soviet Union continued to stream westward. There were continuing reports of mass deaths and labor camps and new stories of the persecution of dissident writers like Anna Akhmatova and Boris Pasternak. Jewish writers like Isaac Babel and Boris Pilnyuk simply disappeared and were presumed to have been secretly executed.*

*Stalin's sphere of power had spread to the states of Eastern and Central Europe. Political manipulation and murder, combined with the threat of Soviet military force, brought Communist parties to power in Czechoslovakia, Poland, Hungary, Rumania, Bulgaria, Yugoslavia, and half of Germany.*

*In the next several years, the new Communist regimes began to conduct purge trials much like those in Moscow in the thirties. Czechoslovakia held a series of trials behind which lay a barely veiled anti-Semitism as former party leader Rudolph Slansky and other Jewish Communists were accused of forming a Zionist conspiracy.*

*At the same time, in Western Europe, particularly in France and Italy, Communist parties subservient to Moscow retained significant followings among intellectuals and workers in large part as a result of their antifascist resistance activities during the war.*

## Irving Howe

The expansion of Stalinist power was a very alarming thing. One totalitarian monster had been destroyed in the war, and for a moment afterward there was a sense of exhilaration, of relief, and now there was another one and it seemed we would never be done with it. The initial event was the Russian invasion of Czechoslovakia and the overthrow of the democratic society there. That was in 1948. When that happened, we felt that it was a dark night again. That darkness was descending over Europe.

## Daniel Bell

Stalin began to twist things tighter. The first open symbol of this was the Slansky trial in Czechoslovakia. Here you had Rudolf

Slansky, the general secretary of the party; Otto Katz, who had been a key figure in antifascist propagandizing and had organized a lot of support in Hollywood; Klementis, the head of the Slovak party; and Artur London all confessing not only to being Gestapo agents as in the Moscow trials but to being in conspiracy with—in league with—Zionist agents. They, along with others, confessed and were executed with only a couple of exceptions.

There was the Rajk trial in Hungary, the Petkov trial in Bulgaria. All these trials were beginning to go on in Eastern Europe. And there was clearly anti-Semitism. There was the disappearance of Mikhoels and the heads of the Jewish antifascist committee, of Bergelson and Markish and the other Jewish writers, and then we learned of the preparation of the doctors plot in 1953, where Stalin's Jewish doctors were accused of poisoning him.

## Nathan Glazer

Communism had extended its frontiers from Minsk to Breslau. They were taking over all of Eastern Europe. There was this fight as to whether Greece would turn Communist or not. There was the Communist victory in China. There was a key election in Italy and one was very much aware the Communist party had 35 to 40 percent of the votes in France and Italy. Where would it end?

And there was the Communist influence on intellectuals in Europe and particularly the French intellectuals, who we were all eager to learn something about after the war and admired because of their brilliance. It was a situation that was terribly worrying in which a false doctrine—one in which the suppression of free thought, of dissident ideas was an integral part—was being spread over more and more of the world.

*Increasingly bitter relations between America and the Soviet Union grew into the Cold War. The Truman doctrine pledged the United States to defend foreign states against Communism. The American Communist party, though much smaller in the late forties, continued to remain active. While it continued to attract idealistic men and women of the left, many of whom were opposed to the Cold War on principle, the party continued to be largely funded by Moscow and its leaders remained subservient to Soviet policy.*

*Hidden from view, the party largely controlled the 1948 presidential campaign of Progressive party candidate Henry Wallace, Roosevelt's former vice-president, who had become an outspoken critic of President Harry S. Truman's Cold War policy. The following year, a Communist-organized Conference on Peace and Scientific Progress at the Waldorf-Astoria managed to attract large numbers of liberal intellectuals and celebrities, ostensibly to support a platform of peace between East and West.*

## Irving Kristol

In the later forties the old pro-Communist, pro-Stalinist left re-emerged in various forms and you had peace congresses which defended Soviet aggression or refused to focus on the threat of Stalinism. The Communist regime was organizing peace conferences in every country and would gather up truckloads of intellectuals. Even after the show trials in Czechoslovakia and Hungary, they swallowed it all. You had an intelligentsia, an intellectual class, that still wanted to believe that the Soviet Union represented the wave of the future and were committed to it—Jean Paul Sartre in France and others in Germany and Britain.

## Irving Howe

The Communists made a major effort at the Waldorf-Astoria conference to bring together intellectuals and people from the Soviet Union on behalf of their views in regard to the Cold War. They brought Fadayev, a literary hack; they brought Dmitri Shostakovich, a great composer. Shostakovich was a pitiful sight. He was clearly terribly unhappy, wanting to be any place else but there. But I guess he had to come. At this conference, the anti-Stalinist intellectuals from around *Partisan Review*—like Mary McCarthy, Robert Lowell, myself—were present and some of us spoke up. They couldn't keep us from speaking.

## Irving Kristol

It galvanized a lot of the New York intellectuals into saying this is
absurd. It's crazy for intellectuals not to be anti-Communist when
all you have to do is look and see what Communists do not only
in Russia but in Eastern Europe. Whenever they come to power,
intellectual life ceases. If you look at what they did in the Soviet
Union, it was very simple: They shot all the poets! There was no
intellectual life in the Soviet Union. None, except that which was
clandestine. Under Stalin the KGB was very good at suppressing
all dissidents. This was a horrible regime in which all of the best
writers died prematurely. The official art was laughable. They did-
n't even produce any good studies of Marxism because that was
too dangerous.

They didn't want thinking people writing about Marxism.
They just wanted rote repetition of Marxist doctrines. And for
American intellectuals or French intellectuals to come here in
New York and celebrate their regime at the expense of our
regime, our system, which had many, many defects, obviously, but
where intellectuals were certainly free to write and criticize, was
an outrage.

*Alarmed at Communism's influence in the liberal community, Kristol,
Bell, and Glazer joined the American Committee for Cultural Freedom,
which had been created by Sidney Hook to organize intellectuals against
the party. Irving Kristol became its first executive director. A constituent
part of the Congress for Cultural Freedom, an international organization
with headquarters in Europe, the ACCF battled what they saw as the
party's continuing respectability in political and cultural circles. Through a
series of publications and forums the committee attempted to battle Communist propaganda over critical public issues, but the party's dwindling
numbers and a growing anti-Communist hysteria made the ACCF a controversial organization in the liberal community. (It was revealed in the
1960s that the Congress for Cultural Freedom and its publications received
much of its funding from the Central Intelligence Agency. One such publi-*

*cation, the English magazine* Encounter, *was at one time coedited by Irving Kristol and Stephen Spender. Kristol denies ever knowing of the CIA connection. There remains a lingering debate over whether CIA funds were used to support the American Committee for Cultural Freedom.)*

## Daniel Bell

The Communist party had in American society very little influence at all. But in key areas—the trade union movement—at one time it had significance. In the intellectual community, and particularly publishing houses, it began to have more and more influence. To a very small extent the universities. Someone from the outside would look at it and say, what's going on here? Why, these people aren't very important. In the society as a whole, they were not. In the culture and the trade union movement, they were.

## Nathan Glazer

It wasn't that the American Communists were the Trojan horse of Soviet Russia—which exercised a real threat. It was rather that they muddied the waters of understanding of what the Soviet Union was and what our interests were, and where we should stand in regard to the Soviet Union. We knew the history of Communist unions, the way they were manipulated into all sorts of positions to support the Soviet Union. That was the problem with domestic Communism, and that's why you had to argue with them.

## Victor Navasky
### Publisher of *The Nation* and author of *Naming Names*

There was no internal red menace. There was an international Communist operation that was run out of Moscow that was invidious, that sent people to labor camps that resulted in mass deaths. The *PR* intellectuals for the most part didn't make that distinction sufficiently. Retrospectively, one would think they were smart enough in terms of IQ and intellectual depth to have made it.

## Irving Kristol

The Communist party of the United States, like the Communist party of all Western European countries, *was* acting as an agent of the Soviet government. They took their orders from the Kremlin as to what to say and what to do. And they were able to mobilize a lot of leading scientists, artists, writers around this program.

Senator McCarthy came along and complicated matters enormously. He was an ally we never needed and never wanted because he was unsophisticated. I don't know if he was even sincere, and he helped to give anti-Communism a bad name. So he was a problem for us. Nevertheless we did not think that to be anti-McCarthy you had to cease in any way being anti-Communist.

*As fears of the Soviet Union rose during the Cold War, opportunistic politicians launched a series of widely publicized anti-Communist congressional hearings. In 1947 the House Committee on Un-American Activities (HUAC) investigated Communist influence in Hollywood. The "Hollywood Ten"—all writers, actors, and directors who were members or former members of the Communist party—refused to divulge their political beliefs to the committee, invoking their First Amendment right to free speech. All were jailed on charges of contempt of Congress.*

*The Hollywood hearings were followed by a series of other HUAC investigations as well as those by Senator Walter MacLaren's Subcommittee on Internal Security. Under pressure from the right, the Truman administration instituted a loyalty oath in 1948 for government employees that was widely imitated at the state and local levels. Soon a number of statewide investigations into the influence of Communism on college campuses sprang up across the country.*

*Fears of anti-Communist political subversion were greatly magnified by the fear of espionage. In 1948, testifying before HUAC, the journalist Whittaker Chambers accused former State Department aide Alger Hiss of spying for the Soviet Union. Hiss denied the charges but was ultimately convicted of perjury. Two years later the Communists Julius and Ethel Rosenberg were arrested, found guilty, and executed for giving atomic secrets to the Soviet Union.*

*In 1950, riding the wave of anti-Communist hysteria, Senator Joseph McCarthy gained national notoriety with his own hearings into Communist subversion in government. A brilliant demagogue, with a talent for manipulating the press, McCarthy made wild, often unprovable accusations in public. During his investigations, he often resorted to an unscrupulous mix of innuendo, bullying, and outright falsehood. Most New York intellectuals were critical of McCarthy and the congressional investigations, but they continued to believe that Communism posed a danger to American political life and kept up a vigorous opposition to it.*

## Nathan Glazer

We were in a situation that seemed similar to war and the Communists occupied positions that seemed something like that of traitors. These were people who, insofar as they had the opportunity, would mislead those who they influenced through magazines, in the union movement, in intellectual life, in the mass media. And we thought the influence of Communists, wherever they were, was pernicious.

So, even though they did not pose a threat to the government—their numbers were too small, the areas within which they had influence were constrained—we were in a dilemma. Our orientation was basically to write articles: You write articles, there will be consequences, and consequences that you, yourself, are not advocating, but others will implement. Did that mean that we, who were opponents of Communism, had been opponents of Communism all the time, had an obligation to hold our tongues?

## Irving Kristol

You must remember the emotion that existed in the United States as a result of the Alger Hiss trial, as a result of all the espionage episodes that had suddenly broken. People began to say, "Hey, there may be Communists in government. We should get them out." So then you have the question, What should we do about Communists in government? We tried to be reasonable about it, but it's very hard to be a reasonable voice when you have McCarthy on the one hand and those who thought Communists were just like us and just had slightly different opinions and shouldn't be discriminated against on the other. We did not take that view. We thought it appropriate under certain circumstances to discriminate against Communists.

*Thousands were called before committees, from party leaders to fellow travelers, to those who had merely signed petitions. Most Communists and former party members used the Fifth Amendment's defense against self-incrimination to protect them from having to reveal any connection to the party, or from having to name others. The refusal to cooperate often cost people jobs and even careers. But Kristol, Glazer, and Bell felt that in deciding not to defend themselves as Communists, party members were once again, as in the days of the Popular Front, hiding their true beliefs in order to gain the support of liberals.*

### Daniel Bell

While McCarthy's charges were wild and exaggerated and in a sense manipulative, on the other side, the Communists were lying. Instead of saying, "We are Communists, and we have a right to be Communists, we defy you. These are our ideas and you are trying to destroy us," they didn't. They fudged. They took the Fifth Amendment or denied.

What the Communists could have done was say, "Yes, I'm a Communist, and I will go to jail for my opinions." In effect, justify themselves as people having beliefs. But they didn't. And they were trying to manipulate the situation by scaring the liberals, by saying, "You see? We're under attack, and then you'll be under attack!"

### Nathan Glazer

We knew that there were really party orders on what to do. The Communist party took the position that people should not reveal their connection.

Now, people could have had their own reasons for taking the Fifth Amendment, to avoid certain kinds of punishments. But the issue was fudged over in the kind of way that we had been fighting against for a long time with Communist front groups. There the issue was who really controls this League for Youth, Democracy, and Anti-Fascism? And why are they taking these positions? We knew who controlled them. We knew why they were taking that position.

Here, in order to be anti-McCarthy, one had to accept the legitimacy of continuing that confusion, that obscurity, that attempt to conceal the relations between Communists and the groups they controlled that we had been fighting all along. So, how could we support that?

## Irving Kristol

The Communists were using the red-baiting very successfully to whip up all the sympathy they could for Communists. If you want to have sympathy for Communists as victims, fine, but say they're Communists and they're victims and that despite the fact that they're Communists, we have sympathy for them. But that's not what people were saying. They were saying, they are victims of McCarthyism. They are innocent. Innocent of what? They're not innocent of being Communists, most of them, in fact.

There was this marshy ground in between, which the Communists were exploiting and which all of us were trying to traverse in different ways using different strategies. Having been a Trotskyist was a great advantage. I understood what Communists were. But a lot of American liberals didn't.

## Nathan Glazer

The problem was the liberals insisted the people under attack weren't Communists, they were leftists, they were liberal, they were radical. People were being attacked for their ideas. Well we know that people were not being attacked for their ideas; they were being attacked for their connection to the Communist party. We rejected the dominant liberal defense of the Communists who were under attack and we couldn't figure out whether to find another defense or to find another attack.

Commentary *proved to be a bastion of anti-Communism within the liberal community. In a now famous essay, "Civil Liberties 1952, A Study in Confusion," assistant editor Irving Kristol argued that outrage against McCarthy's attacks on political dissent had blinded many liberals to the fact that the Communist party and its members posed a problem for the United States. "There is one thing Americans know about Senator McCarthy," Kristol wrote. "He, like them, is unequivocally anti-communist. About the spokesmen for American liberalism, they feel they know no such thing, and with some justification."*

### Philip Selznick
### Sociologist

Irving made a big mistake. He exaggerated the extent to which liberals in general had become susceptible to being fellow travelers, who as it were, were the Communist virus. I think the conclusion was a defense of McCarthy. The mistake was in not realizing there were a very large number of other liberals who certainly didn't come under that category, and it was wrong to seem to join this liberal bashing when, in so far as people had to be criticized, they ought to be criticized more specifically.

### Irving Kristol

I was writing an article attacking fellow-traveling liberals, fellow-traveling journalists and intellectuals who were using McCarthy in order to justify their pro-Russian, anti-American attitudes. I could easily have written five or six more sentences which would have been more belligerently anti-McCarthy. It just never occurred to me to do so, and it never occurred to the people at *Commentary* who read the article to suggest that I do so since they knew I was anti-McCarthy. I did not disassociate myself from McCarthy as vigorously as I should have. I referred to him as a vulgar demagogue. I thought that was enough. In my circles, and certainly at *Commentary* magazine, being anti-McCarthy was taken for granted.

## Daniel Bell

I remember the article very well, because I said to Irving—we would read each other's pieces—"Take out the sentence, it's too provocative." And Irving would be, "Ah . . . phttt." You've talked to him, he's rather flip sometimes. I had a better sense than Irving, how this would play and I said, "Look, it's unnecessary."

## Irving Kristol

It's interesting. Norman Thomas thought it was a fine article. He was a socialist leader. But a lot of the liberals thought I should have made my position clearer. And a lot of liberals thought this is no time to attack liberals. We should all get together and just attack McCarthy, which was the Communist line. But that was not our line, and it was not my line. I mean I wanted to be free to attack liberals even while I'm attacking McCarthy.

These were liberals who were foolish about Communism. In no sense were they really pro-Communist. They were just very foolish about Communism. They didn't understand what it was. They just didn't think that Communism was any kind of threat to anything and they did not seem to be much concerned about what was happening in Eastern Europe, did not seem to be concerned with what was happening to the people in Russia. They were foolish. And so I attacked them and ever since then, people referred to my article as a pro-McCarthy article, which of course it wasn't.

*Though also anti-Communist, Irving Howe felt that his fellow New York intellectuals, in their attacks on Communists, were overlooking the danger McCarthy posed to civil liberties.*

## Irving Howe

Kristol knew that McCarthy was a thug. He knew McCarthy did-n't use nice methods, and McCarthy wasn't someone with whom Kristol would have wanted to associate personally, but the anti-Communism of the moment was becoming so uninflected, so coarse, that it even found a kind of backhanded apology, if that's the phrase to use, for McCarthyism.

My friends and I had no fondness for the American Communists. Politically, we were bitter opponents, but we took, in the 1950s, a strict civil libertarian position. We were against all the persecutions of the Communists. We felt it was playing into their hands. We felt it was a violation of American traditions and principles. We looked upon McCarthyism as a thing of ugliness.

*Weighing in on the controversy, Nathan Glazer wrote an article for* Commentary *as well, this one more clearly an attack on the senator. "It would be . . . correct to classify McCarthy," he wrote, "with those out-and-out demagogues who appeal to passions which they themselves do not hold, or do not take seriously. But . . . at this place and at this time it would not be an exaggeration to describe Senator McCarthy as the inventor of a new technique of distortion . . . what Richard Rovere calls the 'multiple untruth'—the misstatement inserted in a parenthetical remark, a subordinate clause, or even an adjective. The virtue of this technique is that it is possible to pack so much distortion into a given quantity of words."*

## Nathan Glazer

I wrote an article in *Commentary*, a strong attack on McCarthy, in which I gave him no quarter at all. Now, I must say, one of the reasons I did it was in order to repair the damage—I wasn't asked to, I did it voluntarily—created by Irving's article. I figured, let's show that *Commentary* can be really anti-McCarthy. I had no use for him at all. I thought that nothing he was doing was of any value. This was not a unique position. It was the position of the presidential wing of the Republican party. But I go back to the old dilemma, does McCarthy mean you stop talking about Communism?

It was the period of the Korean War. It was the period in which we were very agitated as the Russians first got the atom bomb and then the hydrogen bomb. It was a troubling time, and it wasn't a time to stop talking about Communism and Communism's dangers because of what McCarthy was doing.

### Victor Navasky

People will tell you that it was possible to be anti-McCarthy and anti-Stalinist. The problem was they were anti-Stalinist—and they denounced McCarthyism in some general way—but they also threw other folks on the left, who had been involved with fellow-traveling organizations or the party itself, to the wolves. And it seems to me that did not help democracy. It seems to me that if one is trying to ask what is a moral, political position for those years, it didn't add up to one.

### Daniel Bell

I don't think that's the real issue. The real issue is the fact that the party took an unprincipled stand against an unprincipled adversary. And they both played each other's game this way. And the liberals were being caught between them. In these congressional committees the visible people were called up and asked to testify. Those who were fellow travelers very rarely. Some may have been hurt? Yes. But if the party had taken a more principled stand, it would have been better for everybody. But they didn't, partly because of the way in which they wanted to utilize the situation, to scare liberals.

We took a stand. And I think we were all very clear, what McCarthy was like. The crucial point, it seems to me, is what is one supposed to do in this situation? Keep quiet? We were, in effect, saying that McCarthy was wrong. And so, in what sense were we legitimizing, or not being aware of the civil liberties?

### Irving Kristol

Sidney Hook and I wrote a letter to the *Times* saying we should start a movement and force Senator McCarthy to resign from public life. That's what I thought of McCarthy. But how you deal with Communism was another matter.

### Nathan Glazer

I think it was a very difficult situation. I am not easy, overall, with the positions we took. Our attack on Communism—showing up the errors of the Communists—was so forceful that we really didn't come to the issue of civil rights and the nature of the attackers.

So McCarthy was terrible and the Communists were terrible. Now, what position do we take towards the fact that they're being cross-examined on their views? They're getting fired from positions, they're going abroad to continue their work, and so on.

It is much easier to write a book describing what happened to these people and how excessive was their punishment in the light of their misdeeds or errors—all which is all true—than it is to explain just what role we should have played in that connection. There was no way of responding to the matter satisfactorily, to reconcile honesty as to our views, as to the affiliations and roles of certain people, on the one hand, with consequences that were not up to us on the other. Should the knowledge of those consequences have led us to take a more restrained view on whether people should be honest with regard to their political views?

Well, in retrospect, we never managed to figure out a good position. By good, I mean not one that was politically defensible but that was respectable and moral and responsive to all the complicated issues raised. And I still don't think we have one.

*Though McCarthyism created an uneasy relationship with official anti-
Communism for all four men, Bell, Glazer, and Kristol continued to support the American government's opposition to Soviet power during the
Cold War. In concert with their deradicalization, this eventually led to a
championing of American society and its values, triggering yet another
debate between the three men and their old friend, Irving Howe.*

### Irving Howe

We had been raised, it seemed, with our mother's milk with the
idea that the function of the intellectual was to stand apart from
the governed institutions of society. To be a critic, even if it meant
being marginal in the world. Even if it meant not being part of
the elite. Being a celebrity. Even if it meant writing for journals
with small circulations. To be consistently a critic and to cry that
the fish stank since many of the fish did stink. In the fifties, this
whole impulse which had been the animating values of the
whole of *Partisan Review* since the middle of the 1930s began
slowly to weaken.

### Michael Walzer
### Coeditor, *Dissent*

Irving had a great dislike for all of the simplifications of political
life, and the Cold War was a great simplification of good guys and
bad guys, and an awful lot of intellectuals bought into the whole
thing. Now, Irving and his associates knew about the bad guys.
They had been anti-Stalinists almost from when they were fourteen, but they were skeptical about the good guys. And they wanted to retain a certain view of American society as in need of radical change. They wanted to continue to be social critics, and they
thought that a lot of the Cold War intellectuals—including their
former friends from alcove one—were, by virtue of being opponents of Communism, joining in a great celebration of America.
And it seemed to Irving an unwarranted celebration. This was still
a place of class inequality, of race inequality. It was still a place in

need of social critics, and that was the role of the intellectual. That's what intellectuals were supposed to do.

## Irving Howe

In 1954 I published an article which had its fifteen minutes of notoriety. It appeared in *Partisan Review* and was called "This Age of Conformity." It was a kind of scattershot attack on the whole intellectual world in New York for becoming too socially complacent, for losing its intellectual independence, its social radicalism, its passion for criticism. It was not met with great fondness on the part of many of the victims of the article.

## Irving Kristol

What Irving Howe was objecting to was the fact that I had ceased being radical, and he didn't apparently feel that this was a convincing argument, so he invented something called conformity. What was I conforming to? To what? I mean, I could never get an answer to that question. To the idea that America was a good country? I had had that belief years before. Of course we were conforming to America. So was he. We were all conforming to America in our different ways. America is a very big and various country.

## Daniel Bell

What I find invidious—I don't think Irving meant it that way, but it always gets put forth that way, particularly from the outside—is a moralistic element. *I* am moral, and *you* are not. I have retained my ideals, and you have not. Well, that's nonsense. Because it assumes somehow that a change in a point of view is a surrender of certain ideals. And I've very rarely found that people, even Irving Kristol, with whom I disagree, have sold out.

Sold out for what? And to whom? People change their points of view. And Irving Howe changed his point of view as much as I have. And in many respects this whole set of questions come out of a sectarian background.

## Irving Kristol

Irving Howe was so badly infected with a left-wing virus that he just couldn't understand how anyone could not be left-wing. But you know the world has been full of a lot of interesting and intelligent people who weren't left-wing, and Irving thought that was all wrong. That if you're an intellectual, if you're thoughtful, particularly if you can write, you have to be left of center. Mind you, you had to conform to the left of center view of what a proper intellectual was. I mean, I lived in the same building with Irving Howe, talk about conformism. Which one of us was conforming? We wore the same clothes, pretty much. I don't know what he meant by saying conformist.

## Irving Howe

The tendency in the intellectual world in the 1950s *was* toward conformity, was toward making peace with the status quo, the status quo of American capitalist society, and I was against that. And in '53 we started a magazine called *Dissent*, which would be a voice of independent socialist thought but not affiliated to any organization.

*Far longer than his friends, Howe had maintained his commitment to radical Marxism. But when, in the early fifties, Howe finally freed himself of his Marxist desire for revolution, he sought to understand the socialist tradition in a new, democratic context. The pages of* Dissent *became a forum for rethinking the idea of socialism in America. Through the magazine, he brought together a community of like-minded and disaffected radicals, still intent on attacking American capitalism and its inequalities.*

## Irving Howe

In 1952 I and a few friends left a group called the Independent Socialist League which had been steadily moving from Trotskyism to social democracy. We felt the day of the sects was over. It was over as far as we were concerned. The old formulas of the Marxist left no longer sufficed. We felt that socialism—the whole socialist idea—was in a very deep crisis, and has remained so over subsequent decades. It was necessary to enter into a new kind of experience, sort of free-lance individual, in terms of starting a journal or magazine which would not have any organizational discipline or any party line.

## Michael Walzer

You know Irving's line, "When intellectuals have nothing else to do, they start a magazine." There was a sense of nothing else to do, nothing out in the world, nothing political, in the old sense of "political," to do. They wanted to rethink the whole socialist project, and they also wanted to criticize American society, hence the name of the magazine. This was the period of gradual accommodation of intellectuals to the Cold War.

They wanted to adopt a critical stance that didn't necessarily depend on a particular view of the future, an independent, critical stance, driven by certain egalitarian and democratic values, to rethink what socialism might mean in the future while opening it to criticism.

## Irving Kristol

I was uninterested in it. I just thought it was utterly irrelevant. Echoes from the past. And I never took it seriously. I never read it regularly and it didn't exist on my horizon. I didn't take *Dissent* seriously. Socialism so far as I was concerned was a dead issue. I didn't read it and didn't pay any attention to it.

## Nathan Glazer

The criticisms of the United States I felt were exaggerated, unfair criticisms. I felt our role in the Korean War was a noble one, a proper one. The notion that the American government is always under attack had to make you think, what was wrong with America, and why is it, if you're a socialist, you're supposed to denounce this country? Compared to what?

There was a kind of piety towards the particular brand of socialism that they were committed to. I recall a review of the first issue of *Dissent*, where I said, "What are they complaining about? And what are they arguing against?" America was some sort of enemy? But what kind of enemy was it? We had fought the Korean War. We were opposed to the Russians.

And they were very intemperate and polemical in a nasty way against people who had already abandoned socialism. They fell into easy Marxist modes of denunciation, "sell-outs," and so on. We were all becoming professors, so I couldn't see why one group of professors should attack another group as "sell-outs."

# 7. The Mood of Two Generations

FOR EVERY HOUR AND DAY THAT PASSES, MORE HUMAN BEINGS,
AMERICAN AND VIETNAMESE, DIE NEEDLESSLY IN THAT UGLY WAR,
AND FOR EVERY HOUR AND DAY THAT PASSES, MORE MEMBERS OF
OUR GENERATION BECOME DESPERATE AND HOPELESS IN THEIR
SEARCH FOR THE DECENT SOCIETY.

—*Paul Potter, Students for a Democratic Society, 1965*

I THINK WHAT MOTIVATES THE NEW RADICALS, AND TO THIS EXTENT
IT'S A POSITIVE SIDE, IS A VERY DEEP MORAL FEELING, DISMAY AT
THE HIERARCHIES OF WORK, AT THE COMPETITIVENESS OF THE
SOCIETY, SOME OF THE MATERIALISM IN THIS SOCIETY. AND ALL
THEIR CRITICISMS ARE PUT IN MORAL TERMS. THE DIFFICULTY IS
THE INABILITY TO TRANSLATE A MORAL CONCEPTION INTO A POLITI-
CAL CONCEPTION.

—*Daniel Bell, 1967*

*By the end of the fifties, Glazer, Bell, Kristol, and Howe had made
notable reputations for themselves. Living abroad in London during the
middle of the decade, Kristol had become coeditor of* Encounter, *a new
magazine of politics and culture that, along with his own writing, had
gained him increasing attention. Howe made his mark as a critic with*
Politics and the Novel, *a collection of literary essays. Glazer's interest
in sociology had led to his co-authorship of David Riesman's* The
Lonely Crowd, *a widely praised book on postwar American society, and
to his own landmark study on ethnicity,* Beyond the Melting Pot,
*written with Daniel Patrick Moynihan. Bell's writing on labor and poli-*

*tics culminated in* Work and Its Discontents *and* The End of Ideology, *a book that predicted the death of grand ideologies like Marxism.*

*Though neither Bell, Howe, nor Glazer had received graduate degrees at the time (Bell and Glazer would later be awarded Ph.D's based on their published work), they all found jobs in a rapidly expanding university system that was finally shedding its cultural provincialism and its anti-Semitism. "When the New Yorkers were welcomed into the universities," literary critic Morris Dickstein recalled, "they began to see the universities as refuges for the kind of free development of ideas that they previously thought could only occur outside the university." The four men had found a place at the center of American intellectual culture. Approaching middle age, they had also become convinced of the limitations of political action.*

*And then, they suddenly found themselves confronted by a young group of radicals springing up on the university campuses they had made home. Drawing inspiration from the southern civil rights movement in which many had participated, the members of the newly created Students for a Democratic Society placed their hope for political change in the kind of direct action taken by young blacks in the South.*

*Early student radicals like Tom Hayden turned to sociologist C. Wright Mills, whose book* The Power Elite *was a piercing attack on the coterie of politicians, businessmen, and military leaders he believed controlled American society. A political romantic, Mills was an admirer of Fidel Castro and his recent Cuban revolution. He quickly became an intellectual icon to many members of SDS who, like him, were deeply opposed to the Cold War and directly at odds with the liberal anti-Communism of the New York intellectuals.*

## Tom Hayden
### President, Students for a Democratic Society, 1962–63

No younger generation likes to feel that it's being lectured to by their parents, ideological parents or biological parents. Especially if they think those parents have a lot to answer to themselves. It's true today. It was true then. They believed that any means were necessary, including military means, to fight Communism abroad. That

was the principal tenet defining you as being a moral and politically correct human being. And, secondly, that New Deal and Great
Society-type solutions—that is, trickle-down economics with a
large welfare state—were great achievements to be honored.

We thought that the Cold War was draining democracy, that
civil rights were not a reality in the South. Poverty in 20, 30, 40
percent of the population was a raging issue that could not be
solved within the framework of the welfare state. And we didn't
understand why they were defending a system that seemed pre-
posterous to us. I think it was because they put their lives into
achieving it, but it's just not in the human cards that people will
thank their elders for something that happened thirty years ago.

## Daniel Bell

Tom Hayden came to see me after he graduated Michigan. He'd
read *The End of Ideology*, he was curious. And he was sort of caught
between Wright Mills and myself—those were his two poles, in a
way. And clearly, he chose Mills. But what struck me most about
Hayden, apart from the personality of the man, which I never
liked—someone once called him the Richard Nixon of the left,
which I think is a very good appellation for Hayden—was that
these were people who had lost a sense of historical memory. The
thirties were sort of lost in the fog, the fifties were confused for
them, and they thought they were coming out of themselves. They
had no feeling for Stalinism, they had no feeling for things we'd
gone through in this way and there was a hubris of being new.

## Irving Kristol

I thought, my goodness, we're getting a replay of an old movie. I
had nothing against those young people. Most of them were
young socialists or would have been young socialists. I thought
their political program was utopian—in and of itself, harmless.
And I thought they had some reason to be upset about the condition of American society. And particularly the conditions of

the universities—which had become huge bureaucratic, impersonal institutions.

But, at its origins it was suburban radicalism, a phenomenon that was alien to me. We were born of the Great Depression. They came out of affluent suburbs, for the most part. Their parents had made it. So the situation was quite different. I mean, we really feel we suffered deprivation unnecessarily because the system should have worked better than it did. Their resentment was much more ambitious. They wanted to change the world. Well, in the end, we decided we wanted to change the world, too, but I think we had better incentive to change the world than they did.

## Todd Gitlin
## President, Students for a Democratic Society, 1963–64

We weren't afraid of the Depression, and in fact, we were sort of tired of hearing about it from our parents. We were the children of the Cold War, not of fascism. We didn't feel the immigrant's sense of relief at having arrived in a country which was supportive, and where you could live. We were more easily revolted by the fatuousness, the plastic quality, the racism of the culture.

The Bomb was a much worse danger to us than any Communist regime. We thought we were in an unprecedented historical situation. We thought the existence of the Bomb set us aside. The Bomb had driven a knife through history, and we were now faced with the possibility of the end of humanity, and therefore, no one who had been born much before us, no one who had a memory before Hiroshima, could possibly understand the anguish we felt.

*Critical of the political status quo, the young Students for a Democratic Society found a target for attack in Daniel Bell's* End of Ideology. *The book's title essay became its most famous—and controversial—piece, its meaning still debated by the author and his critics today. Part analysis, part prognostication, Bell's piece proclaimed that the era of grand, all-encompassing Marxism, fueled by religious, messianic passions, had come to an end, finally laid to rest by the disaster of the Soviet experiment.*

## Daniel Bell

I've said repeatedly that people always hunger for an emotional creed. And therefore, there will always be a search for new ideologies to that extent. If one conceives of ideology as a kind of joining of a world map with a mission, there will always be these kinds of hungers. The crucial point I was trying to make was that up until the 18th century, roughly the French Revolution as a kind of symbolic turning point, most of the politics were basically cast in religious terms. You have religious wars. Even though there were political interests, the terminologies were religious. What you have after the French Revolution was a crossover, namely that terminology was now political, but often the impulses were religious: messianic, eschatological, apocalyptic. And what I was saying with *The End of Ideology* is that the impulse in which you now had purely a political terminology for these religious impulses was probably finished intellectually.

*Bell did not lose sight of the fact that politics would always involve conflict over the means and ends of public policies that were necessarily rooted in moral values, but many felt that his book had emphasized managerial technique, downplaying the need for a larger vision.*

## Todd Gitlin

We certainly were damned sure that we had ideology, we thought it was a good thing, and we were going to prove him wrong. The notion that ideology had ended, was to me, at eighteen or nineteen, not only offensive but unfair. It was as if he was saying, we're pulling the rug out, kids, we're shutting up shop. You don't get a chance to do ideology on your own. It's closing time.

## Tom Hayden

President Kennedy, in one of the speeches that we least liked, said, I think in 1962, that it's no longer about ideology, it's about technique. That came from Bell's book and books like it, that basically said society was no longer—and this was partly a factual assertion, but also they wanted this to be so—divided along ideological lines. We took that to mean not any longer around moral lines.

Well, we're looking at five thousand people in jail in the South for civil rights violations that they shouldn't have had to go to jail to have enforced and we're wondering how can anybody sitting in New York, or anywhere in an academic chair, be saying society is in an equilibrium? It didn't make any sense to us.

## Todd Gitlin

Liberalism thought that the world was basically okay, at least the American world was basically okay, except for, to use a phrase of the times, pockets of poverty. Basically, America had produced an honorable, a decent way of life and there were a few more people to let into it, we should open the gates and let the outsiders in to our party, but our party was a dandy party. You all come.

## Irving Kristol

You can refer to a liberal establishment which dominated the universities. There's no question about that. But that they did not protest in favor of civil rights for blacks, absolutely untrue. I mean they were the ones who supported all the liberal candidates. They were the supporters of Hubert Humphrey who brought the Democratic party into the civil rights struggle. So it's not fair to them. They did not take direct action, that's true. It was for the blacks to take the direct action. And the blacks did it and it worked because public opinion smiled on them. But the reason public opinion was so favorable was because of this liberal establishment that spent quite a few years making it so favorable.

*The elder generation had long been disenchanted with a romantic view of politics, the result of their own experience of radicalism and their long and bitter fight against Communism. "They had come to a much more hard-bitten, pragmatic, reformist view of society," as literary critic Morris Dickstein explains. "These young radicals of the sixties came along with a resurrection of what they thought were naive, romantic, utopian, moral visions." To Bell and Kristol, SDS's cherished ideal of "participatory democracy" with its quasi-anarchistic vision of a society ruled harmoniously by its citizens seemed hopelessy unrealistic.*

## Tom Hayden

The phrase "participatory democracy" came from a professor of philosophy in Ann Arbor, Arnold Kaufman, who was kind of a mentor to many of us. I think it was a label that helped us enormously in trying to give some theoretical foundation to what we were talking about. All it really meant was a greater emphasis on direct democracy from the bottom up, instead of representative democracy where you rely more and more on incumbent politicians or bureaucrats to solve your problems for you. But it was also a style.

It meant that movements were more important than bureaucracies, and people were more important than experts in generating the conditions for social change, and it meant that movement organizations should be participatory, rather than hierarchical. This put us squarely in the tradition of Native Americans, Quakers, Transcendentalists, Romantics, and all kinds of populist traditions in America. Our parents had built some material opportunities for success that the world hadn't seen, but had left us without identity or without a spiritual anchor in a world of trouble. Participatory democracy gave us a certain base to argue from, morally and politically.

## Daniel Bell

"Participatory democracy"—the idea that people ought to have the right to control the decisions which affect their lives—sounded fine. But then when one said to them, well, tell me, if you have a southerner who doesn't want to break up his life and accept blacks, or, as in Boston, you have people in the Southie [South Boston] who don't want blacks to come in, do they have the right to affect the decisions which affect their lives? There was a lack of complexity in their political ideas, but they had a certain passion and emotion behind it—an understandable one.

### Irving Kristol

I never believed in it. It's an old left-wing romantic idea that Rosa Luxemburg wrote about prior to World War I, which Hannah Arendt wrote favorably about in some of her writings. Participatory democracy works fine in very small communities. Very small uniform communities. Very small conformist communities, like the Israeli kibbutz. If you believed in what the kibbutz stood for, were willing to accept their style of life and not challenge it, yes, the participatory democracy worked in the kibbutz. But of course it only worked up to a point because people got bored with it. But it's certainly of no relevance to the American nation.

### Todd Gitlin

Participatory democracy was a break against any conventional idea about how to pursue politics. It was a way of turning on a conventional assumption about the relation between talk and politics. Participatory democracy was an idea that talk was good for self-rule. Freedom is an endless meeting. But I think the tremendous appeal of participatory democracy was to the idea of a unitary experience of community.

　　I can understand why the elders thought this was naive. You cannot conduct foreign policy this way. You cannot even conduct economic or welfare policy this way. You can't run a factory this way, you can't run a school this way. And it was virtually impossible to run an organization this way. You couldn't even run an office this way. All of that was true. But there was a romance attached to it, and I think that was why so many of us, for a while, were attached to it. It brought life together, all as of a piece. It was a response to the impersonality, the bureacratization, the abstraction of life.

*Still suffering from their years of isolation in the fifties, Irving Howe, unlike his friends, saw in the rise of the Students for a Democratic Society the possibility of political renewal. In SDS lay the hope for a rebirth of the left in America and a potential ally in their own radical struggle.*

## Irving Howe

In the early sixties, relations between my gang, the group around *Dissent*, and SDS were quite good. We were sympathetic to the idea of participatory democracy and the idea of participatory democracy still has a certain force to it. That representative institutions tend to rigidify, become formalized, and you go through these elections every four years, you pick a candidate, but that most people don't really have any share in the actual decision making in the country. In participatory democracy there was an effort, a little naive to be sure but an effort, to find ways to allow people to participate more actively and steadily in political life. They had a fraternal, liberalistic, socialistic view with which we could easily be in harmony.

## Michael Walzer
## Coeditor, *Dissent*

Arnold Kaufman was a regular *Dissent* writer, and Kaufman was a significant mentor of the SDS group, which I'm sure was one of the key reasons why they were interested in meeting with the *Dissent*ers. And we were very eager to meet these kids. So there was a lot of hope. It's a feature of a group like the *Dissent* group, that even though they were then in their thirties and forties, they start looking for successors early on. Political movements need to reproduce themselves, and especially movements that have their origin in Marxism. There's a very strong sense of the thrust of world history. Who will come after us, and who will carry on this political tendency?

### Todd Gitlin

We wanted some sort of confirmation. They wanted, I think, also, some sort of confirmation and so five SDS leaders met with five *Dissent* editors in a mansion right off Central Park. I know that several of us, at least on the SDS side, came with a sense of reverence, and antagonism, combined. These were the fathers we were meeting with, and at the same time, they were the proprietors of the left, such as it was. When I interviewed Irving about it, in the mid-eighties, he spoke about the tension they felt because they wanted so badly to find us and to contact us, and to be redeemed and continued by us. But as he also recognized, they over-reached. We all did. There were so many expectations crowded into that little room, that it was very easy for a flame to ignite a lot of inflammable material.

### Michael Walzer

Irving had devoted his life to trying to understand and to combat what was, in his eyes, the great betrayal of the Western left by the Communist leaders. It had to be the case that he would ask these young people, "What is your attitude toward the Soviet Union and the international Communist movement? What is your attitude toward the revolution in Cuba, the Maoists in China?"

Those issues just had to loom large in his head. And these kids didn't have the same experience. They didn't have fully formed views, and they resented what they thought was an insistence that they recite a catechism.

### Tom Hayden

It was very puzzling. If you said, "I think students should have the right to vote, I think students should be able to write opinion pieces in the Ann Arbor paper without them being censored, I think black citizens in the South should be able to vote, I think we should desegregate the South," if somebody then said, "but how anti-Communist are you?" it would just seem they were on another planet.

## Irving Howe

We quarreled over Cuba, the Castro regime which they defended, I think foolishly. They had romantic notions about Castroism as being a better form of Communism than that in the Soviet Union and I think history has shown they were totally wrong. Some of them seemed to us very authentic and idealistic, and sincere.

We also sensed important differences among some of the SDS people. Perhaps the most gifted among them, Tom Hayden, was someone we felt had a very strong authoritarian, manipulative streak. We could see the commissar in him. And that put us off.

## Todd Gitlin

Tom was defending nonviolence. And Tom at that point was an absolutist about nonviolence. And Irving was more or less baiting him: "Could you love a fascist, Tom?" Tom insisted that he could, and to Irving this was incomprehensible. When he heard Tom's toughness, what he saw as Tom's posturing as a hero, he heard Stalinism. But, as he realized years later, Tom was not that. Tom was an American moralist, in the tradition of the abolitionists, in the tradition of Emerson and Thoreau.

I don't remember a vein popping, but Irving was certainly angry and he was harsh. Marty Peretz, who was a student of Irving's, said Irving was a "brutal debater," and he meant that as a compliment. I think it was true, and I think he was really revolted by what he was hearing. And he was unrestrained in his expression of that revoltedness.

## Tom Hayden

I was not raised in, thankfully, a household of people yelling at each other about the correct line, so I couldn't comprehend the decibel levels that these people would reach. And also, they reminded you, in a sick way, of your father. This was paternalism beyond Abraham—paternalism to an extreme that I've never heard of. People pointing at you and lecturing to you. They didn't appear to be doing anything. And we were going to jail. So at least we knew we were on the right track.

I think the root issue was that we were homegrown in response to a situation in front of our eyes and they were trying to transpose a world view from the past onto the present and interpret everything through that lens. So, some leader of SNCC [the Student Non-Violent Coordinating Committee, the nation's leading student civil rights group in the 1960s that would later lead the Black Power movement] would become, in their eyes, consciously and above all subconsciously, a new Lenin. Whereas we just thought it was Stokely Carmichael. It would never occur to us that we were incarnations of previous menacing figures.

## Michael Walzer

I had also encountered early on the old-left polemical style, which was very harsh, impersonal. You were supposed to come back the next day and start the discussion again. Irving was enormously talented at that sort of thing, so when he slashed, the wounds were deep.

## Irving Howe

Probably we made a lot of tactical blunders. Some of the criticism they made of us now and even then, we saw had a certain validity. We tended to seem to them people who knew everything or thought they knew everything.

We had become a little fixed in our views, a little rigid in our postures. It's something that comes with age the way your bones and muscles become rigid. We were impatient; we scolded. At the same time we wanted to influence them. And we were hurt by their assaults upon us.

## Todd Gitlin

I certainly thought that they'd become frozen in their thought. And it was the freezing of their thought that had encapsulated them in a kind of inaction that we were eager to extricate ourselves from. Their thought had led them to a bitter-end conclusion that the world was signed, sealed, and delivered, had (in terms of social possibility) been engraved in granite, in the thirties and forties. Stalinism was a conclusive refutation of revolutionary possibilities. We, being spry and vibrant fellows and women, would get out of those traps. They were reconciled to being marginal intellectuals who had politically failed, and while they were honorable, we were going to surpass them, because we were committed to being popular. We were going to be winners.

## Irving Howe

There's an inevitable conflict between generations but I think that to reduce the differences between them and us to a generational conflict is a superficial way of looking upon it.

## Michael Walzer

Irving saw something more than just the refusal to recite a catechism, than just the generational conflict. He saw a group of young people who, because they were unwilling or unable to learn from his experience, from other people's experience, were going to repeat the mistakes of the left, were going to be seduced by Che Guevara. He saw it all, and it's quite amazing how accurate it was. He later came to regret some of the acrimony of this prophecy.

But the prophecy itself, of Tom Hayden and North Vietnam,

the prophecy was so accurate, the picture that they were heading in a direction which would make it as difficult for them to be independent and authentic American radicals as it had been for leftists in the grip of the Soviet Union.

*Nathan Glazer arrived at the University of California a self-described liberal with radical tendencies. Disenchanted with government bureaucracy and in favor of small-scale community reforms, Glazer had also protested against the nuclear arms race. At Berkeley, he was naturally drawn to a group of students engaged in a series of civil rights demonstrations against Bay Area hotels and car dealerships.*

*But, the following year, the student protests led the university administration, under pressure from trustees and local businessmen, to enforce a seldom-used ban on campus political activity. Students were prevented from organizing and recruiting on school property and the university became a target of protests over the right to free speech. Suddenly, Glazer found himself in a batttle with his former allies.*

## Nathan Glazer
When I came to Berkeley in 1963, I still thought of myself as a man of the left and for the first few months of the free speech issue, I was on the side of the free speech people. The students I was closest to were people who believed in organizing. They were all committed to the civil rights movement. I thought that was a good thing, too. They were committed to what they felt was right. They were a remarkably good group. But there came a time when I felt that the push against institutional authority was simply excessive.

## Jackie Goldberg
## Leader, Free Speech Movement
When I first met Nathan Glazer, I was in absolute awe of him. I'd read his books. I thought, *"Wow, this is my advisor! Big time!"* I thought that he was extremely bright, and knew a tremendous

amount, and I was a little afraid of him. He was a person who pursued a lot of issues that I was very interested in, including educational reform. As time went on, it became apparent to me that we had a major philosophical difference. First we would chat about it. And then, we would argue about it. And he was decidedly angry and hostile. He thought we were wrecking the university, destroying the university. He kept saying to us, "Well, I may agree with your goals, but not your means of achieving it." And the bottom line is we were serious students. And we were treated by the Nathan Glazers of the world as if we were not. And that was insulting.

## Nathan Glazer

They were being treated very well, had a very good deal. They were at a great university—it was practically free—and the degree of their discontent was disproportionate to the situation, disproportionate to the point where one distrusted their own bona fides. Is this really bothering you so much, or are you after something else? The basic issue, as I saw it, was institutional authority, and an institutional authority that in no way was suppressing free speech. The university had certain rules about where you should hand out literature and where you should collect money, and where you could organize for your march on downtown Oakland or whatever it was. And I felt these were legitimate rules.

## Jackie Goldberg

There were a lot of people who felt very strongly that it was an attempt to say that students at a major university did not have the right to participate in the social and political life of the country. This was about the ability to be involved in the social causes of the day. I mean, there was a presidential campaign aloft, and the Young Democrats and the Young Republicans were banned equally with the Trotskyists, the Communists, the socialists, and everything in between. We thought that was a basic First Amendment issue.

I felt almost betrayed. Not that they [Glazer and other faculty] had ever made a commitment to me, but it was a commitment that I had felt from their ideology.

## Jack Weinberg
## Leader, Free Speech Movement

What we saw as a noble effort to be part of changing American society, and making it more just and making it more equitable, and tearing down the color bar, was viewed by the business community as attacks and the university ended up taking sides, taking the wrong side from our perspective. I came to the university thinking "this was truth, this was wisdom, this was knowledge." There was a higher place. The civil rights movement was righteousness. Suddenly we found out that the university was on the wrong side.

*Administration resistance to the call for free speech on campus convinced protesters that direct action was the only means of changing the university. Angry students soon occupied the school's main administration building. A university administrator stepped into their midst. The demonstration had "developed to such a point," he declared, "that the purpose and work of the university have been materially impaired." Long frustrated with the university, students cheered in triumph. Nathan Glazer and fellow City College radical Seymour Martin Lipset became two of the Free Speech Movement's most vocal opponents.*

## Nathan Glazer

Something emerged—a kind of enthusiastic and euphoric rejection of forms and norms. Nothing was happening that justified such a response. I felt they were demonizing the administration of the university. There was an aspect of—almost of a taunting, of seeing to what extent one could put this institution and its representatives off-balance, which was not a legitimate way to conduct the argument or discussion, unless one thought it was such a reprehensible institution that anything you did to show it up was correct.

They felt that their basic principles were being denied them, but what was strongest in my mind was the sense of disproportion, I mean, their whole notion of trying to equate students with workers and being oppressed by the machine! They were living in this beautiful environment, and nothing much was being asked of them. The thought was ridiculous, and yet that was part of their rhetoric.

## Seymour Martin Lipset
## Professor of Sociology, University of California

At one point, Glazer and I spoke from on top of a police car. The car had come into Sproul Plaza [which lay in front of the administration building and became a main site of the protests] and the students had surrounded it and wouldn't let it move so the cops finally gave up and left. It became an impromptu soapbox. Mario Savio [a leader of the FSM] got up on it. Nat and I got up and were arguing against the civil disobedience. I made the argument that civil disobedience is warranted if you don't have a democracy or if you have a severe evil, and an evil in which there were no democratic mechanisms to get rid of it. But that wasn't true in this case. One, the evil wasn't that great, and secondly there were other ways of protesting and trying to change it.

*Over the course of the fall, the continual arrest of students, their limp bodies dragged time and again by police into paddy wagons, proved, as students had hoped, eerily reminiscent of their civil rights protests. Though a compromise was reached between students and administration, allowing students to organize and speak on campus within regulated times and places, in truth, a psychological breach had opened that would only grow worse as the decade wore on, in campus after campus across the country.*

## Jackie Goldberg

Their view was, lift your voice, take pen in hand, write a letter to the editor, speak in Congress, stand up and be heard, and if the system says no, you say, "Well, win some, lose some." We thought that was just bankrupt. Because the issues were more important than a wonderful debate in your living room. The issues were life and death.

The liberalism that they espoused was an armchair intellectual liberalism. Think the right thoughts, talk the right words, hang out with the right people, but you shouldn't really get your hands dirty, because if you get your hands dirty, then God, it could get out of control! They were control freaks. The last thing in the world you ever wanted is for something to maybe get out of control. Terrified of the mob. But you know, in a democracy, when you're afraid of the mob, you're afraid of the people. Because in a democracy, you don't have to have a mob. We can vote. We can speak.

### Nathan Glazer

That split was decisive. There were certain key issues which regardless of any other position you had, made you conservative. And the key issue that labeled me a conservative, labeled a number of us as conservative, were the student unrest issues of post-'64. And it didn't matter if you were against the Vietnam War, which I was. And I wrote articles against it, joined groups against it. And it didn't matter that you were against nuclear escalation. And it didn't matter that you were for the war against poverty and more expenditure on the poor and so on. All these things became irrelevant, and certain things became crucial. Just like today, a position on affirmative action becomes crucial. Nothing else matters. Call yourself what you will. That is what will determine who you are. And there came a time when there was no point in arguing with it.

*By 1965, seeking to prevent the spread of Communism, President Lyndon Johnson had committed troops to fight in the Asian country of South Vietnam against its northern Communist rival. Over the next several years, United States troop strength increased, as did the deaths of young American soldiers. A small antiwar movement soon began to rapidly expand, catalyzing SDS and turning it into a mass movement among the young. Thousands protested the war across the country, and by 1968, antiwar sentiment forced Johnson to abandon his race for another term. Frustration with Johnson's liberal administration and growing anger over the Vietnam War turned many student protesters violently against American power. A small group of radicals turning toward the old Marxist theories of the left began to blame American capitalism and American society for the war.*

## Nathan Glazer

The Vietnam War was a very painful, difficult situation, but when the young critics of the Vietnam War—and I was a critic all the way, from the very beginning to the very end, wrote articles, joined organizations, and so on—looked at the matter as some kind of attempt of American capitalism to save itself, I thought that this was just stupid.

We thought the United States on the whole was a good society. It may have taken us a while to get to that point, but we did. We thought its political structure was right and we thought its economic structure was sound enough. We thought its opportunities for the poor and the underprivileged and minorities were extensive and were right and we thought it was moving in the right direction of extending these opportunities.

When we saw this attack launched in the most extreme terms, we simply didn't understand what they were arguing about or what they were fighting about. The critique they launched of the United States was something we simply could not accept. And yet they had gone through a process whereby they had moved to this kind of extreme criticism, which then also began to extol violence as a way of getting rid of this terrible society.

## Irving Howe

We felt very strongly that by 1968 or so, the New Left people were not engaged in intellectual dialogue or debate or political struggle with us. They were out to destroy our bona fides. They were out to deny that we had a right to exist.

The New Left spoke of confrontation. It was not as if they were confronting the board of directors of GM. They were confronting, most of the time, liberal professors. They were choosing very much their own targets. They were confronting precisely the people they should have been trying to form alliances with, who had in fact a certain sympathy with them, at least initially. We were against the Vietnam War, but we around *Dissent* had no illusions about the regime in North Vietnam.

The differences became very sharp and very acute, and I had some bitter, difficult experiences on various campuses where I was booed by the New Left, which did not exactly develop into civility of discourse. Their confrontations were a form of sectarianism and they suggested a spirit of intolerance that would only end in self-destruction.

### Tom Hayden

From 1968 to 1970, there was an increased sense of rage. I think it accumulated over the previous eight years and I think it was based on a sense that there wasn't going to be any reform, it was just now a clash of wills, and to a certain extent, it was necessary to say or do dramatic things for the purpose of the media. Theatrical politics begin to dominate. And much as I feel remorse about some of those things, because I think anger is the least pleasant human emotion, it doesn't really have anything to do with the question at hand. The question at hand is whether it was correct to defend the status quo against the students. If you enforce the status quo with policy consistently enough, over and over again, it is going to raise the emotional level until you get sheer acts of physical confrontation.

### Todd Gitlin

The university was simply not, any longer, the quad of disembodied learning. It was something else. Something had happened in the country. Universities had become integrated into the Cold War system of power, research, and deceit.

*Located on the Upper West Side of Manhattan, Columbia University had become a kind of unofficial annex of New York intellectual life. By 1968, Daniel Bell had been a Columbia professor for ten years. Lionel Trilling, perhaps the country's preeminent literary critic, also taught there along with former* Partisan Review *editor F. W. Dupee, the historian Richard Hofstadter, and the art critic Meyer Schapiro. That spring, years of student anger against the war suddenly erupted on campus.*

### Daniel Bell

Columbia in the sixties had been a remarkable school. People like Hofstadter, Trilling, Meyer Schapiro. It had a glow, had intellectual excitement. What is a university if not that? It's not a vocational school, it's not a training school. It's a place of intellectual debate. Yet all this was simply kicked away and by kids who had come out of nowhere.

### Tom Hurwitz
### Member, Students for a Democratic Society, Columbia University

Columbia University had a way of containing within it most of the problems in American society at large. It was a microcosm. In the spring of '68, we saw a university that had for twenty years trampled on its neighbors in Harlem, evicted people from their homes, which was also the largest defense contracting university. We were against the war, we were against inequity in society, but we had in our own administration an example of what was worst about our society, and we could confront it by confronting it right at home.

*That spring, the university's long-standing plan to build a gymnasium in a public park in Harlem provoked accusations of racism from radicals in the Columbia branch of SDS and in the Student Afro-American Society. In*

*April a protest at the gym site led to the spontaneous occupation of five campus buildings. Students demanded that the university abandon the gym and sever its long-standing ties to a think tank doing military research. Bell felt that the students' actions posed a serious threat to the intellectual life of the school.*

## Daniel Bell

There was no sense of compromise with the radicals. They had no sense of the university as a community. The university's a very fragile institution. There are very few institutions which have that degree of continuity which allow for discussion, debate, free exchange of ideas. And to assume that it's only a manipulative instrument of the ruling class is ludicrous. There are elements of it—the reproduction of the class structure—all this is partly true. But to take the university as a target, that it was complicit with what was all wrong with the world, was ludicrous. It was easy and cheap and I resented this.

## Diana Trilling
## Wife of Lionel Trilling, Columbia English Department

There was no idea about anything in the campus uprisings as I knew them. There weren't any ideas at all. It was just, as Dwight Macdonald put it (he said it in praise!), shove society. It was an attack on authority. The only idea that animated the campus uprisings was to challenge the established authority, whether of your institution or of your society as a whole. That was what you had to challenge.

## Paul Berman
## Member, Students for a Democratic Society, Columbia University

I thought they were deaf, they were deaf above all to the panic that was spreading among the students about the war in Vietnam and the moral panic in regard to the civil rights revolution and American racism. There was an idea that a kind of latent democratic community spirit could be invoked which may have contained within it an attack on authority but was in itself a larger idea than merely attacking authority. It was an idea of establishing some new kind of healthier community and unless you understand that aspiration you cannot understand the exhilaration that swept through so many thousands and thousands of students in the course of the uprising.

## Tom Hurwitz

The senior faculty were very privileged members of the university and tended to see it in only positive terms because they loved their positions at the university. The idea of criticizing it, and the idea of looking at the whole situation, especially at Columbia, was really beyond them, because they benefited so thoroughly. And I think their whole attitude toward society was, in many ways, determined by their relationship to the university.

They could be liberal in relation to the Vietnam War, but when the university itself was criticized, then their very privileged position was also shaken, and they reacted like most privileged people do when their position is shaken.

## Daniel Bell

I remember at one point a student saying to me, "Who are you to tell me what to study?" I said because you don't know what you don't know. If you knew what you didn't know, you could go out and study. That's what I'm here for, to show you what you don't know. If I can't do that, I shouldn't be paid. But they didn't even understand something as simple as that.

*A week after the occupation began, Bell and other faculty attempted to negotiate a peaceful resolution with the student radicals, but failed to reach a compromise. Furious with the intransigent students, President Grayson Kirk and Provost David Truman finally called in the police.*

*Many professors used their own bodies in an attempt to barricade the buildings against the use of force. Though the black students were given the chance to quietly leave Hamilton Hall, the four buildings occupied by white radicals were stormed. Angry blue-collar policemen showed little mercy for the Ivy League student rebels.*

### Daniel Bell

I remember coming back after a discussion with David Truman, dean of the college, and saying, "Look, whatever you do, don't call in the police. The police will simply come in and riot and break heads. You have to go ahead and argue with them. I just had a debate with a man named Szymanski about Marxism and sociology, Lionel Trilling had a debate." I said, "You have to go and argue with them."

He said, "I'm not going to argue with those kids with their temper tantrums." I said "Look, David, you can't assert authority, you have to earn authority." He said, "Nonsense."

### Tom Hurwitz

The police were brought on campus, and beat us, and sent us to the hospital by the hundreds and sent us to jail. And if that hadn't been so coherent with the policy of Columbia administration throughout its entire tenure, we would have been shocked. But we weren't shocked, we were just enraged.

### Daniel Bell

I can only tell you, when that happened at two o'clock in the morning, Lionel Trilling and I walked down the hill—he lived on Claremont Avenue, I lived on Riverside Drive—and I came home and burst into tears.

### Diana Trilling

They couldn't do an ordinary commencement that year. They couldn't do it at the university so they did the commencement at St. John's Cathedral, and they also did another commencement up in Riverside Church. I went up to Riverside Church. The president of the university could not speak, it was so dangerous; he was so much under attack. And Richard Hofstadter, the historian, went up to speak and he spoke about what was the point of an attack on the best thing that our society could offer us which was education. It was very moving, deeply moving, and I think I wasn't the only person who began to cry.

## Paul Berman

What finally caused so much damage to individuals and even to the university was the horrible and fateful error of calling in the police. However willfully excessive had been our own behavior, the discussion had been moved to the plane of brute violence. Many of us felt that it was the university administration and not us who had betrayed the ideal of the university.

## Daniel Bell

The events of 1968 destroyed Columbia. SDS was ready to destroy the university because they thought the revolution would come. Their tactics, it seems to me, were totally nihilistic and destructive. It tore the faculty apart, destroyed Truman's reputation, it left a reign of bad feeling. A lot of us left afterwards. I'd been offered a job at Harvard before and I'd said no, but afterwards there was so much bad feeling I said it's hard to live here.

## Irving Kristol

I recall one of the leaders of the student rebellion at Columbia writing an article in which he said, "You don't know what hell is like unless you're born in Scarsdale." Now, Scarsdale is a really nice place. All the world wishes it were born in Scarsdale. In a way the American dream is to create more Scarsdales. And I thought that was a very revealing and pointed remark. And a very poignant remark as well.

It showed the limits of success in our public policies which could leave behind a spiritual vacuum. I think that spiritual vacuum pervaded our suburbs. I think it pervaded our universities. America is a bourgeois, secular, capitalist society. The capitalism part is fine. The liberty part is fine. The secular part created problems. And I think we're beginning to understand now what those problems are. People feel a vacuum in their lives.

## Todd Gitlin

I think there was something going on which was maybe not so fully thought out—and it was part of a larger tendency, within the movement of those years—to think that we could go it alone. Because liberalism was fundamentally tainted, because institutions seemed fundamentally corrupt, because normal American life seemed so barbaric, or fatuous, or unsatisfying or unsexy, or stultifying that if you succeeded, in style, in culture, in way of life, in temperament, in relationships, that you could, in a sense, found yourself a new nation. And that nation would fight, as nations had traditionally fought, for self-determination. By toughing it out. I think there was this subterranean sense that it was possible to start the world all over again.

## Irving Howe

The most tragic consequence of the New Left was what it erased. There was a very great deal of idealism among tens of thousands of young people. Some of it remains, but a lot of it has been destroyed. A lot of it has died out and gone sour. It also, I think, created a very bad series of political backlashes. These kids had an extraordinary gift for knowing how to use and manipulate the American mass media. They were probably responsible in some sense or to some degree for the election of Richard Nixon. The New Left were the ones who created an atmosphere in which people reacted strongly against it and ulimately turned to the right.

# 8. The Neoconservative Revolt

> I BECAME RADICAL BECAUSE I THOUGHT I HAD A GOOD REASON TO
> BE RADICAL. I BECAME LIBERAL BECAUSE I THOUGHT I HAD A GOOD
> REASON TO BECOME LIBERAL, AND THEN I BECAME CONSERVATIVE
> BECAUSE I THOUGHT I HAD GOOD REASON TO BE CONSERVATIVE.
> SEEMS TO ME PERFECTLY NATURAL.
>
> —*Irving Kristol*

*Even as a younger generation of radicals were attacking the Democratic party for its resistance to change, Irving Kristol, Daniel Bell, and Nathan Glazer had become convinced that liberals were trying to produce change too quickly. Promising a war on poverty and inequality, Lyndon Johnson had initiated a host of government social programs. The three men felt that the Johnson administration's liberal beliefs—its ideology—had obscured an awareness of the limits of what social policy could achieve in curing poverty and social ills.*

*Bringing together a group of like-minded intellectuals, they began a new magazine,* The Public Interest, *in 1965. Using the methods of social science, they set out to examine the consequences of government policy, hoping to have an impact on the politicians and bureaucrats who made it.*

## Irving Kristol

The 1960s were full of big ideas, most of them fantasies, and we decided to have this magazine which would take a very realistic, somewhat skeptical view of social policy. I and Dan Bell and Nat Glazer, we got together and started *The Public Interest.* The only thing I could think to do. I didn't run for office. We started a magazine—on a shoestring.

*The Public Interest* was, in its origins, still a liberal magazine but without a liberal ideology. We had a circulation of a few hundred to begin with. That didn't bother us. With a circulation of a few hundred, you could change the world.

## Daniel Bell

Being ideological means you have prefabricated ideas. You cut and trim the ideas to fit the formula and insofar as we were trying to show that these problems were probably much more complex than people realized—needed some kind of database, some more thorough analysis—it had to be nonideological. It wasn't the explosion of myth, it was the idea of taking a cool look at public policy and finding out how complicated it was.

## Nathan Glazer

It was strictly limited to a discussion of domestic policy, on which we felt we could be more informed, could draw more from the social sciences than was being done at the time. We felt that it was possible to bring more knowledge, more understanding, even more science, to social problems.

## Irving Kristol

We were very skeptical of most of the Great Society programs. I thought the war on poverty, as constructed then, was very foolish. I knew poverty, I knew what made poor people tick. They were listening to the wrong kinds of intellectuals who didn't understand poverty, and had very grandiose ideas about how to move people out of poverty. And they were using the wrong ways to solve those problems. I discovered all sorts of what seemed to me to be crazy things happening in these programs: distributing money to the poor even while the income tax system was taxing the poor.

The question is how do you lift people out of poverty? How do you lower the crime rate? How do you improve the quality of life? What do you mean by the quality of life? These were the kinds of questions we were addressing. And I still think that the legitimate question to ask about any program is, "Will it work?" I've learned that you have to be very careful with that question. You really have to ask it many times over and not be satisfied with an easy answer

## Daniel Bell

With any welfare reform, school reform, housing reform, etc., problems exist. We ran a piece about a Johnson program which tried to build a model housing complex for the poor on government land. He thought, "I'll show those liberals!" and the idea was that there would be no problem because it's government property, they don't have to buy anyone out, they can do what they want with it. Well they immediately ran into environmental hazards, environmental problems, and then of course the people who abutted the land didn't want the housing. There are all these problems that plague reform, but the virtue of being a left-wing intellectual is that all you need is the idea, all you need is the slogan.

One of the very first pieces in *The Public Interest* was by Adam Yarmolinsky, who had been one of those responsible for shaping the war on poverty in the Johnson administration. Adam wrote an article in which he said, "It's very easy to have ideas. It's harder to translate ideas into programs. It's harder to translate the programs into policy. It's even harder to translate policy into legislation. It's hard to translate legislation into institutions. And it's harder to get the institutions going toward the objectives you had in the first place." But people stop at that level of the ideas alone.

## James Q. Wilson
### Professor of Strategy and Organization, UCLA; contributor to *The Public Interest*

We felt the Community Action Program particularly, urban renewal programs, Medicare—these were all signs to us of government being heavy-handed about achieving objectives that most of us didn't quarrel with. Nobody was in favor of poor housing or uncared-for elderly people. We just thought that these were clumsy mechanisms.

And we thought that the role of social scientists in public policy—and I still haven't changed my mind—is not to advise presidents, not to whisper in the ear of the candidate, but to sit down and figure out whether a policy that the government is undertaking will or will not achieve the results the government has stated. You had to try to persuade policymakers to take seriously some understanding of human nature in advance so that you would realize how complicated a phenomenon it was when they tried to change it, that changes have consequences.

## Nathan Glazer

You have to think about what has happened over the years. For almost any of these social issues, there's something deeper involved than just a shift in government policy.

It was true that when New York was poor, it had one-tenth as many people on welfare. How were *they* managing? There were charity societies, there were private organizations, and there were friends and family. But they must have managed poorly. Now, you'd think, they must be managing much better. Think of the sums involved. But are they managing much better?

I don't want to idealize the past but there is a tendency to replace other charitable mechanisms. This is what government programs do and they become part of a general, large change in the character of society, replacing traditional institutions that were still playing a role in keeping things together.

Programs with the best intentions can fail to have the effects intended. And there were not only programs that failed to work, there were programs that also had negative consequences. With welfare [a New Deal program that greatly expanded in the 1960s] women knew that if they had children they would get some degree of support, if they had more children, they would get more support. And they would not need husbands for this purpose. Clearly that's a big change in society. One may want to approve it from the point of view of giving women freedom to have children without husbands or without makng sure they have male support-ers, but nevertheless it did create a change. And now that we're try-ing to reverse it, we see how difficult it is.

## James Q. Wilson

I suppose the slogan of *Public Interest* authors taken collectively is "the law of unintended consequences." At the time, I was worried about crime. Criminology was much seized by the idea of crimi-nal rehabilitation, and I was struck by the fact that there was scarce-ly any evidence that rehabilitation worked. And criminology was more or less convinced that deterrence didn't work, and I began to see evidence that in fact deterrence did work. The general liberal policy on crime was, in my opinion, bankrupt. That is to say, first they would deny that the crime rate was going up. We had ample evidence from citizens directly that the crime rate was going up, and they were mad about it. Secondly, the continual emphasis on eliminating the root causes of crime, a strategy which was at that time intellectually empty, because we didn't know what the root causes of crime were, and to the extent we could guess, like weak families, for example, there was no government program around that was going to change it.

*For the disaffected liberals around* The Public Interest, *affirmative action became a critical example of the "unintended consequences" that often grew out of large-scale social policy. Lyndon Johnson first forcefully advocated the idea of affirmative action in a speech written by Daniel Patrick Moynihan (who would become a key contributor to the magazine) at Howard University in 1965. "You do not take a person who for years has been hobbled by chains," Mr. Johnson explained, "and liberate him, bring him up to the starting line of a race and then say, 'You're free to compete with all the others,' and still justly believe that you have been completely fair."*

*Created as a temporary means of redressing long-term discrimination against blacks in companies doing business with the U.S. government, affirmative action spread to colleges and universities, state governments and the private workplace, ultimately growing to include other minorities, as well as women. For Bell, Glazer, and Kristol, many affirmative-action programs, in trying to remedy discrimination against blacks and other minorities, undermined the principles of fairness and the rights of the individual. The attempt to achieve equality of opportunity by assuring access to jobs and education for minorities had, in their eyes, been transformed into a desire to achieve fixed results at a steep cost to society.*

*Their opposition to affirmative action, crystalized in Nathan Glazer's 1975 book,* Affirmative Discrimination, *proved to be one of their most controversial political stances, with many in the liberal community viewing them as retreating not simply from affirmative action as a policy, but from the goal of racial equality itself.*

## Irving Kristol

At the beginning we were not hostile. We said why not make up for past injustices, why not give blacks a little leg up? We never thought in terms of hiring unqualified people. We just thought of pushing the qualified people toward the head of the list. But pretty soon it became clear that's not the way it worked. When quotas emerged, when suddenly universities were being told you have to get more blacks in your student body, in your classics department, more in this department—I said that's not the way we want our educational system to run.

## Nathan Glazer

I began to object to the fact that specific race and ethnic categories were brought back into public policy against the specific language of the civil rights act. They were brought back positively, not for discrimination against blacks, but I thought the agreement was no quotas, no account of race, a race-blind society. And I think that was the understanding on both sides, and almost immediately that changed and I objected to it. In my book *Affirmative Discrimination*, I dealt with the issues of employment, admissions to higher education, school busing for racial proportion, and housing, where there were a few government efforts to ensure that there would be mixed housing. And in each case I thought this was unnecessary and counterproductive. I felt that the effects of nondiscrimination would be such that blacks would, as other ethnic groups had, find their place in the larger society.

## Daniel Bell

I always had the feeling that to some extent affirmative action was necessary. Going back to the original Pat Moynihan speech for Johnson, you don't start the race equally between blacks and whites because they haven't had the same advantages. You have to back the disadvantaged. So for prudential reasons you have to have some degree of affirmative action. But then you should realize that you're not doing it as a principle, you're doing it as a prudential fact.

Initially affirmative action was based on discrimination. When blacks still weren't doing well, it shifted to the idea of representation. But representation became too tricky because it's identified with quotas and they're unpopular, so then the rationale became "diversity" without any real thought. You can argue diversity, but it becomes a code word for quotas. It's been an underground process. And I've always resented the fact that policy issues which should be openly debated on their merits and on their prudential effect just slide by.

It's a very tricky question: How much do you bend the rules? I've always had the view that, in principle, it's not a good idea for society. There have to be standards. And most of the supporters of affirmative action want to talk about how to get into the system, but not about standards.

*The critique of sixties liberalism by the founders of and contributors to* The Public Interest *was joined to a critique of the counterculture and what they saw as its destructive influence on the morals and values of American society. Their belief in the limited effects of social policy was echoed by a complementary belief in the need for moral limits. The Modernist vision, which they had once seen as a liberating force against the spiritual dead-ness of the Communist party and a decaying capitalist culture, was viewed in a new light. In the years since their deradicalization, they had grown to appreciate the importance of American cultural and political traditions that they believed were fundamental to the country's stability and its political freedoms. The embrace of the idea of liberation—moral, sexual, or drug-induced—imported into the counterculture from Modernism through the fifties Beat writers was seen as a deeply troubling phenomenon.*

## Irving Kristol

The idea behind sixties radicalism was an attack on all authority. I thought it was an outrage that young people should behave the way they were behaving. I never believed in student revolutions. Every student revolution the world has ever seen, every student-led revolution has been a disaster, because students don't know how to govern. They're pretty good at revolutions but they're terrible at governing. How could they be, they don't know anything.

## Daniel Bell

There was a hubris of being new. In many ways it was a great con-ceit. It was a conceit in the sense that what they were doing was repeating what happened in Greenwich Village before World War I. If you read the history of Greenwich Village before World War I, you see the same phrases, the same ideas, the same word "new," that dreadful word "new" which allows you to do anything—without regard. I believe in condition, I believe in continuity, and I believe in judgment.

## Paul Berman
### Journalist

A spirit arose to question traditional structures of society and private life and to ask whether any given social role was something that ought to be maintained or abandoned and this kind of questioning took a thousand forms. It took the form of, Are haircuts necessary? To have a proper home is it necessary to live in a place that looks like a proper home? Out of this questioning came some bad answers, but also came some very good questions that led to excellent answers: Is it necessary to maintain the hierarchical relations between men and women? Is it necessary to go on persecuting and reviling homosexuals? Doesn't the civil rights movement pose a cultural problem as well as a narrow problem of legal rights? And those were all very good questions that led to novel answers that they, at the time, were incapable of appreciating.

## Daniel Bell

In many cases there was a struggle for rights and that's a valid and genuine struggle, because people were being denied various rights. We were always for equality. That it is essentially a male culture, yes, that people are denied rights, yes. If people wanted to be homosexual that was their right, it never became an intellectual problem for any of us, though it would be later for Irving Kristol. The fundamental point is that there was implicitly, sometimes explicitly, the notion of no restraints, that anything possible should be realized and that sanctioned the acting out of impulses and gratifications. The very word liberation had echoes. It had echoes of emancipation, echoes of slavery, it's part of the mythos of patriarchal domination. Liberation from what and to what?

## Irving Kristol

The sixties radicals were antinomian, against the military, against political institutions, against university institutions, against the family, against everything. It's still with us because it fits in so neatly with American individualism. It can be made to look as if it's simply an extension of Whitman or Ralph Waldo Emerson. But it's not.

### Todd Gitlin
### Sociologist

They were able to find a form of thought that corresponded to what a lot of people were feeling. Namely, the country's being torn apart by these disrupters, by these marginal people, by these super radicals, by the sheer pressure to change. You know, be a feminist instantly, be a radical instantly, be an antiracist instantly. The *Public Interest* writers arrived with a body of rhetoric, and in some cases a body of thought that was serious. I don't mean to say that it was right. But it was serious. It took seriously the fact that a lot of people felt disgruntled by this convulsion of the sixties.

*Recoiling from the effects of sixties radicalism and the counterculture, and increasingly critical of liberal social policy, Kristol, Glazer, and Bell found themselves on the margins of liberalism. In 1972, under pressure from radicals, the Democratic party was moving further left. The antiwar presidential nominee, George McGovern, pledged an expansion of the social programs begun under the Great Society.*

### Diana Trilling
### Literary Critic

Just before we went to Europe in 1972, Gertrude Himmelfarb— who is Mrs. Irving Kristol, as you know—phoned to ask whether we would give our names to an ad in *The New York Times* for Nixon in the '72 presidential election. He was running against McGovern. I had much criticism of McGovern but I wouldn't dream of giving my name to Nixon, and neither would Lionel, but this ad ran and there were Democrats in this ad, "Democrats for Nixon." This very thing was the beginning of the neoconservative movement, and they went on to become a very vocal force in American life with the Republican victory in the White House.

## William F. Buckley, Jr.
## Publisher, *National Review*

Years after the event, Irving Kristol wrote that he had picked up a newspaper in which he saw advertised what one could buy a house for in Levittown. And he saw it was $23,500. And then he looked quite coincidentally at an article that then described the efforts of the federal administration to encourage the rebuilding of apartment units in the Bronx and in Queens and discovered the cost per unit was higher. It was not much later than that, that he gave birth to the notion that he'd been mugged by reality.

## Irving Kristol

In the sixties crime became a problem. Drugs became a problem. I found myself, without even moving all that much, more of a conservative and less of a liberal. I began to see that not just the left-liberal answers, but the official liberal answers were inadequate and have been inadequate ever since. One had the sense that the liberal impulse was out of control.

After all, look at 1972. The Democratic party moved left. It was no longer the party of Hubert Humphrey. It was the party of George McGovern. And the Republican party moved center after Barry Goldwater. It was no longer the Goldwater party. Nixon was no Goldwater. I found myself getting more and more disillusioned with what then was regarded as the official liberal position. Even on the basis of what works, one was forced to become more conservative.

In the mid-seventies I decided, to hell with it, and I reregistered as a Republican. After all, Pat Moynihan was in Nixon's cabinet, Henry Kissinger was in Nixon's cabinet. A lot of the cabinet or subcabinet people I met were perfectly reasonable, intelligent people.

*Bell found himself arguing more and more about issues with Kristol until their disagreements came to a head over the 1972 election. Despite misgivings, Bell ultimately supported McGovern and, soon thereafter, quietly left* The Public Interest. *Glazer, like Bell, remained a Democrat, but continued working with Kristol, and replaced Bell as an editor of the magazine. Over the next decade, neoconservative influence helped create a resurgent conservative movement, culminating in Ronald Reagan's election to the presidency in 1980 and a rightward shift in the American political landscape.*

## William F. Buckley, Jr.

Was there an infusion of energy on the right? I think there was. It seems to me that the expertise associated with sociology was introduced by this set of people with some force, in the sixties and seventies. The neocons taught the conservatives—they certainly taught me—methods of the organization of social data, which I wasn't familiar with. The conservative message at that point had become so platonic. It was all about "morals," this is how people *do* behave, rather than relying on an accumulation of data based on what people actually do.

## Norman Podhoretz
### Editor, *Commentary*

The idea of limited government, the idea of equality of opportunity, the emphasis on the individual as opposed to the caste or the group, these are all traditionally liberal ideas and these are the ideas that are supported today by people called conservatives. The basic truth is that the fundamental values on which this country was founded as expressed in the Declaration of Independence, in the Constitution, in the writing in *The Federalist Papers*, used to be called liberal. And it is wanton and reckless to tamper with them, as many people now called liberals are always eager to do.

## Michael Walzer
### Institute for Advanced Study, Princeton University

They weren't—or most of them weren't—egalitarians anymore. They weren't asking with every one of their proposals, what effect is this going to have on the social hierarchy and on the way peo-

ple relate to one another on deference and arrogance and humili-
ation in everyday life.

They had a strange combination of Burkean conservativism
about how you really can't do very much with state action, that
there are radical limits on the effectiveness of all these programs
and a growing enthusiasm for the free market. But of course, the
free market is the most radical social force at work in the world
today, as it was then. It is, as Marx says in *The Communist Manifesto*,
the force that overturns all habits and customs and continually
transforms everyday life. It seems to me that increasingly the neoconservatives were in the grip of the ideology of the free market.
And they seemed to me to be Bolsheviks in the way they adopted
and defended and promoted this ideology. It was as if all the old
bad habits had come back. Well, maybe they weren't such bad
habits. In the political world, they worked, apparently.

# 9. Two Cheers for Utopia

> WE LIVE IN A TIME OF DIMINISHED EXPECTATIONS. . . . IDEALISTIC
> VISIONS, UTOPIAN HOPES, DESIRES FOR SOCIAL RENOVATIONS ARE
> ALL OUT OF FASHION—INDEED, ARE REGARDED AS DANGEROUS ILLU-
> SIONS THAT SET OFF MEMORIES OF TOTALITARIAN DISASTERS. . . .
> THE CURRENT CATCHWORD IS SOBRIETY, WHICH SOMETIMES LOOKS
> LIKE A COVER FOR DEPRESSION. . . . [BUT] UTOPIANISM IS A
> NECESSITY OF THE MORAL IMAGINATION. . . . IT IS A TESTIMONY TO
> THE RESOURCEFULNESS THAT HUMANITY NOW AND THEN DISPLAYS
> (TOGETHER WITH OTHER, FAR LESS ATTRACTIVE CHARACTERISTICS).
> . . . IT IS A CLAIM FOR THE VALUE OF DESIRE. . . . SO TO FRIEND
> AND FOE, AT A MOMENT WHEN THE EMBERS OF UTOPIANISM SEEMS
> VERY LOW, I'D SAY: YOU WANT TO CALL US UTOPIANS? THAT'S FINE
> WITH ME.
>
> —*Irving Howe*, Two Cheers for Utopia

> EVER SINCE I CAN REMEMBER, I'VE BEEN A NEO-SOMETHING: A
> NEO-MARXIST, A NEO-TROTSKYIST, A NEO-LIBERAL, A NEO-CONSERV-
> ATIVE, AND IN RELIGION ALWAYS A NEO-ORTHODOX, EVEN WHILE I
> WAS A NEO-TROTSKYIST AND A NEO-MARXIST. I'M GOING TO END UP
> A NEO. JUST NEO, THAT'S ALL. NEO-DASH-NOTHING.
>
> —*Irving Kristol*

*In the years after the neoconservative revolt, the political landscape contin-
ued to be dominated by the political right. The strong conservative movement that Reagan had reinvigorated and then ridden to power continued
to control the Republican party and the American political agenda
throughout the eighties. Liberalism was in retreat, the word itself seemingly*

*unutterable for any viable Democratic candidate. Bill Clinton's presidential victory in 1992 put only the second Democrat in office in twenty-four years. But his election was proof that the Democratic party had undergone a signifcant transformation during those years. Clinton's victory had been engineered by centrist forces within the Democratic coalition eager to shed the politics of the sixties left-liberal coalition, but the election of a strongly ideological Republican Congress in 1994 dedicated to the further retrenchment of the postwar welfare state produced a political environment sharply polarized between left and right.*

*Meanwhile, the fall of the Berlin Wall in 1989 and the overthrow of Communism, first in Eastern Europe and then the Soviet Union, ended more than forty years of Cold War and signaled the triumph of democratic capitalism. The complete collapse of these formerly Communist regimes, rather than a long-hoped-for reformation was a devastating blow to many on the democratic left. Within an increasingly narrowed but volatile American political universe, the four men found themselves locked once again in a debate over the country's future.*

## Irving Howe

In the coming decade or so the political struggles will no longer be between the East and West or between democratic capitalism and Communist totalitarianism. It will now be a struggle between conservatism—Thatcherite conservatism or Reaganite or Kristolite conservatism—on the one hand and social democracy on the other.

## Irving Kristol

You get social justice in the hands of the government, and it's in the hands of ambitious politicians. And it becomes a profession. Social justice should not be a profession. I believe we should encourage people to do what they should do to help people, to the degree that people can be helped. And to the degree that they can't be helped, they can't be helped. There's a certain harshness about the neoconservative view of social justice. But I believe our obligations to help people do not extend to those who refuse to be helped. You can't help an alcoholic who wants to remain an alcoholic. You can't help a drug addict who wants to remain a drug addict.

For me the critical turn in the new conservatism that has emerged and is still not fully grown was when Ronald Reagan praised Franklin D. Roosevelt. That represented a sharp break not only in the Republican but in the conservative tradition. I did not accept Goldwater as being the righteous conservative. I never have.

We neoconservatives were never against the New Deal. Never against many of the programs of the New Deal. Never against some of the principles of the New Deal. We are against an intrusive and overbureaucratized federal government.

## Nathan Glazer

Some of my best friends are Republicans, but I don't feel, as Irving often does, that it is important that the Republican party triumph, that the party is a valuable interest. He has a commitment to conservatism as a political movement that I do not have.

Maybe I'm more nonideological. It may be that on many issues I come down on the side of the Republican party, but it will be for different reasons than Irving would give, and certainly not because this will hurt the Democrats and be good for the Republicans.

It's true, I do have a certain vision of a healthy society and community, but I don't think that a terribly consistent set of issues and positions emerges from that.

*In the nineties, Daniel Bell was driven to reassert his liberal political beliefs in the face of the newly powerful conservative movement. At the same time, he held fast to his longtime self-description as a liberal in politics, a socialist in economics, and a conservative in culture. His later scholarly work has drawn on a tradition going back to Marx, attempting to grasp the essence of social change in the contemporary world. In his 1973 book,* The Coming of Post-Industrial Society, *he foresaw the crucial place of technical and specialized knowledge in a world increasingly dependent on information for economic growth. He issued a new edition of the book in 1999, in the midst of the changes wrought by the growth of the Internet.*

## Daniel Bell

You ask me if I'm a neoconservative. What I find amusing is that people who decry a one-dimensional view of society, a one-dimensional view of politics, apply a one-dimensional label to things.

I think I've been consistent all the way through. It's not that my politics haven't changed. Politics is basically a response to particular situations. I think my fundamental values have remained, and my fundamental view of understanding society has remained.

I believe there are different realms in the society and there are different principles which underlie these realms. That's why I've called myself a socialist in economics, a liberal in politics, and a conservative in culture. I'm a socialist in economics because I believe that every society has an obligation to give people that degree of decency to allow them to feel that they are citizens in this society. In the realm of economics, the first lien on resources should be that of the community in a redistributive way.

I'm a conservative in culture because I believe in continuity, and I believe in judgment. I don't believe that all opinions in culture are the same as everybody else's opinion. I don't believe that all art is the same. Some things are better than others, and you have to justify why it's better than others, and you have to understand the grounds of justification.

I'm a liberal in politics but liberalism has no fixed dogmas. It has no fixed points, that you can say, "This is the liberal position." It changes because it's an attitude. It's a skepticism. It's a pluralism, it's agnostic.

*In the last decades of his life, Irving Howe continued to write steadily on literary subjects from Emerson to T. S. Eliot. In World of Our Fathers, his acclaimed 1976 study of Jewish politics and immigrant life, he found his way back to the vanished culture of his youth, discovering there the source for his own continuing socialist beliefs. Howe made his peace with America's traditional party system, helping to found the Democratic Socialists of America in order to press for change within the Democratic party. With the bitterness of the sixties beginning to ebb, he found himself reconciling with a number of his old foes from Students for a Democratic Society.*

## Michael Walzer
## Coeditor, *Dissent*

All of us at *Dissent*—and Irving has been one of the most persistent in this—hold on to socialism by continually redefining it, rethinking it. We have sponsored a long series of articles on market socialism which would once have been thought to be a contradiction in terms. Socialism was supposed to lead to a withering away of the state and the abolition of the market. We now talk of a socialism that makes its peace with decentralization rather than straight, top-down economic planning.

Why cling to socialism? I think the answer has to do with a sense of a historical tradition. The central vision of a society of equal men and women, who participate, who join together in shaping their own destiny, that is a socialist vision. It has been carried on by a succession of socialist parties and movements, and I think Irving's view has been that one doesn't want to be the end of that line. One doesn't want to give up on that project.

## Irving Howe

We continue our criticism of the injustices and inadequacies of a society which allows thousands of people to be homeless in the streets, an affluent society in America where there is still a vast amount of poverty, social dislocation, social pathology.

The crucial lesson of the last fifty years, one crucial lesson is the absolute indissolubility, the absolute organic connection between democratic practice and socialist hope. The great tragedy of the last half-century has been the enormous waste of idealism and energy which the Communist movement represented and its malappropriation of the socialist vocabulary, the socialist idea. It will take a good deal of time before the consequences of this are undone.

But socialism means a greater social ethic, a concern for the needs of human beings, economically and culturally—a gradual transformation from the ethic of accumulation and me-ism to social sharing. All of this may sound vague at the moment, I guess it has to be.

## Todd Gitlin
## Sociologist

I started reading *Dissent* again in 1972 when I was looking for a way back to rational politics. I kept up with Irving's work and at some point we had a few fugitive contacts. By the early eighties I felt very much in harmony with most things he was saying and thinking about the world. I didn't actually see him until I went to interview him for my book on the sixties and as I left his apartment after doing that interview, I realized that I was at that moment exactly the age that he had been in 1963, the year when we SDSers had our little confrontation with him. No small thing.

By that time, I felt very much that the *Dissent* group was my crowd. This was basically the world in which I was having my political and cultural arguments. It was just a matter of time before they asked me on the editorial board. It had been my intellectual home, to use an old SDS phrase, for quite some time. *Dissent* has now lasted for forty years and that's not easy to do. We're in the margins but that's simply the fate of a certain kind of thought in America.

## Irving Howe

Our goal is toward the continuous extension of the welfare state, toward greater social provision in the hope that there will be an eventual transition—not guaranteed but desired—toward social fraternity and social equality.

To me, socialism is no longer a dogma or ideology, but it is a vision, a hope, an expectation for the world in which there will be greater equality and a common ownership of major industries. Not nationalization, not government ownership, but shared ownership by the people who work in those industries.

*Over the last two decades, Nathan Glazer's work has been instrumental in helping reshape the social policy debate in Washington. Informed by a pragmatic sensibility, his approach to issues has produced a body of political ideas often caught between the liberal and conservative worlds. Paraphrasing Glazer's own description of another social analyst, one might easily say that "his contribution to our understanding of [public policy lies] in his avoidance of anything so grandiose as a vision." In his 1988 book,* The Limits of Social Policy, *he scrutinized the failure of government welfare policies. At the same time, Glazer has recently reversed his longtime opposition to affirmative action out of a fear that its abolition will lead to a resegregation of higher education.*

## Nathan Glazer

I have been a critic of liberal social policy, but I've been a critic more in regret than in triumph. In that sense I maintain much more of an affiliation with the world of liberal social policy than other people who are called neoconservative. I write for the Urban Institute. I look at policies that try to improve welfare. I think that almost everything can help a little. It doesn't solve the problem, but perhaps it means that, of these thirty-two families who have received this kind of assistance, sixteen will be better off than they might have been otherwise.

But have I become a pessimist about the ability to change

society? Yes. There's no way of getting away from that. I approach almost any change with the general orientation that it will do less than you think, except for very small changes.

As far as affirmative action, I think that in principle I am for a color-blind society and I think the Constitution calls for it, and I think that even black thinkers want it, but certain things that I thought would happen did not. If someone had asked me in 1965, where do you think blacks will stand in education thirty years from now if there are nondiscriminatory means of admission to institutions of higher education, to professional schools, I would have thought that they would stand more or less like other groups, that it would not be a problem. But it was a problem because they did not. Why this has happened is partly a mystery and partly a result of the history of discrimination. But I think what happens in practice, without the aid of affirmative action, is too hard to live with, so I have changed my views. For other areas—busing, housing, in the case of employment—I'm opposed to government action, though I think it's legitimate for private firms and businesses to have preferences for blacks and other discriminated groups.

In the end, I don't think social policies can necessarily affect the problems that concern us most deeply, like the disorganization of the poor. But I do think that you must keep on trying, even if you haven't had great success. I suppose there is a tension there, but I find it hard to find a simple reconciliation of this tension. I think that I am now more concerned with countering evils than promoting good. I am concerned about issues like equality and poverty. I don't quite know what to do about these. But it comes to a point where at least you have to start talking about it. As inequality keeps on increasing, at least you have to return to the problem and ponder it.

*In the seventies and eighties, Irving Kristol, through his connections to corporations and foundations, was instrumental in funding and promoting conservative intellectual thought, helping to create a new generation of writers and thinkers. His own ideas proved extremely influential in the*

*Reagan administration, and he became a powerful behind-the-scenes figure in the Republican party during those years. Among other topics, his essays have explored his belief in the importance of traditional morality and religion, championing the growing political participation of religious organizations, including the religious right.*

## Irving Kristol

The notion that a purely secular society can cope in purely secular ways with all the terrible pathologies that now affect our society has turned out to be false and yet we have rendered religion impotent as a social force. I really think religion has a role now to play in redeeming the country, in doing something about the high rates of illegitimacy, the high rates of venereal disease, the high rates of AIDS, alcoholism, and drug addiction.

I don't say that religion can solve it all. Not on its own. But you can't keep religion out of it. You must give religion a role in these matters which involve spiritual discipline and personal self-definition or else they will fail.

I remember early on, five or six years after *The Public Interest* was founded, we were discussing how the war on poverty should be launched. And I said why in God's name did the war on poverty insist on forming new groups in the ghetto—political groups—to receive the money, but not give it to the churches? Why not use the churches to cope with welfare and all of the other problems that Great Society programs are supposed to serve?

I was told you can't do that, it's unconstitutional. I don't know whether it is or not but if the Supreme Court persists in saying that it's unconstitutional, obviously the Constitution will have to be changed or the courts will have to be changed or both. I think it is utterly ridiculous to exclude from a good society the one organization which is most effective in bringing about a better society. And liberalism is not prepared to give religion a role. Conservatism is, even if it doesn't know how to do it, and that has made me culturally conservative.

## Daniel Bell

Well, unfortunately, in terms of my own sense of it, Irving's become completely ideological. If anything by now, this is the radical difference between us. Irving's become ideological in the sense that it's become a crusade for him and therefore he's become more aggressive in his point of view. Fair enough, but it's more of a crusade rather than a skeptical examination of issues.

## Irving Kristol

I don't know whether that's true or not. It's hard to see this sort of thing about oneself. I have become interested in trying to develop a conservative agenda. I think that in democratic politics, with societies in flux as they are, you do need an agenda to keep up with change. But I don't think that's ideological. Applying what you have learned from decades of experience I don't regard as ideological. I don't think I have become an ideologist. I accept certain principles of political philosophy or social philosophy which perhaps I didn't accept twenty or twenty-five years ago. But I don't regard that as ideology.

I still regard myself as being a neoconservative, to the degree that they still exist as distinct from conservatives. I still regard neoconservatives as being very pragmatic, while having learned a great deal about social theory and social policies. I don't know why Dan calls me ideological. What I meant when I said the Republican party should become more ideological, which I think I may very well have said, is that it should have an agenda to cope with change and if necessary, to inaugurate change.

## Daniel Bell

He did an article in *National Interest* about a year and a half ago which absolutely made me gasp. He said, For me the Cold War is not over, to me it's now a war against liberalism. And I blink. I say, well, I can be critical of liberalism, but a war against liberalism? Why?

Well, "Liberalism is responsible for the moral decay of the

country," and this I find quite wrong. It's true that one of the weaknesses of liberalism is that it's hard for it to set limits, it has a certain permissiveness. But to say a war against liberalism seems to me quite wrong.

If one talks about the moral decay of the country, none of those people on the right have said very much about what I think is one of the most grotesque forms of moral decay in the country: in the ethics of so many of these business corporations. The way they've basically lived lives of total luxury and spoliation. Not a word of condemnation of this. Moral decay is always the poor blacks, homosexuals, and others as a form of family values. Nothing on the other side. This I find to be quite wrong. Liberalism is not responsible for these grotesque elements of modern capitalist behavior. I find myself at a 180-degree difference.

As I say, I think Irving believes this. It's stupid to say he's doing this for political purposes. Irving has thought through certain kinds of arguments and he believes this is a way of stopping what he thinks is the moral decay of the country. Yes, there are elements of moral decay but look at the other side of that coin, too.

## Irving Kristol

If you were to ask any liberal in 1960, we are going to pass these laws, these laws, these laws, and these laws, mentioning all the laws that were passed in the 1960s and '70s, would you say crime would go up? Drug addiction would go up? Illegitimacy would go up? Or will they go down? Obviously they would have said they will go down. And everyone would have been wrong.

That's not something the liberals have been able to face up to. They've had their reforms. And they have led to consequences that they did not expect and they don't know what to do about it. Conservatives are only slightly better off in that they don't bear responsibility for the reforms but at least they're willing to look at them. There's still a lot of work to be done among conservatives in creating some sort of agenda for a decent society.

*More than fifty years after first meeting in the City College cafeteria alcoves, Glazer, Kristol, Bell, and Howe had yet to give up the hope of molding the world more closely to their still passionately held visions of the future. Visions of revolution had long since faded, and dreams of the good society were troubled by an awareness of society's seemingly intractable problems. But in their continuing attempts to change the world, they were still willing to hold out hope, to give, in Irving Howe's words, at least "two cheers for utopia."*

## Nathan Glazer

It is assumed when you deal with people in the academy that engagement is not necessarily part of their work. They are professional. I feel when I read something by Bell or by Kristol, I am reading something that counts more than when I read other things. Now, if you were to press me and say, "Why does it count more?" Well, in part because I know them, I know where they're coming from, I know where they're going to. I respect them. All of those things are part of it. But it simply counts more. I know it's not just another kind of professional inquiry or something of that sort. I suppose the assumption is, the involvement is a passionate one.

## Irving Howe

A lot of American intellectuals made fun of us for being so oriented to Russia. They were partly right. But they were largely wrong because the essential question which dominated our generation was the question of Stalinism. This has been the essential problem of political intellectual life in the twentieth century. That may be a simplification, but I think it's true.

Here was this terrible, brutal, horrifying dictatorship which had risen out of socialist sources and which used the socialist vocabulary, which appropriated Marxism to itself, which was a kind of travesty, a parody of our hopes and desires. How could we cope with this? How could we understand it and what could it mean?

Is there a tie that binds all the people that fifty years ago were in alcove one at City College? With people like Danny Bell and even someone like Nat Glazer, even though he's quite a bit to the right of us, I do feel very strong ties. I have various disagreements with Bell, but I feel a strong tie with him. With Kristol I feel no longer any tie whatever. He has gone way over to the other side. He's a spokesman for corporate interests, for the Republican party. I look at him as a political opponent. And the fact that we were together fifty years ago doesn't stir the faintest touch of sentiment in me. I wish him well personally, a long life—with many political failures, I hope.

## Irving Kristol

It's interesting. The four of us were all Jews. We were all from New York but not quite the same background. Irving Howe came out of a secular, socialist Jewish background. I did not. I came out of an Orthodox Jewish background.

Socialists have always liked the prophets more than the rabbis. The prophetic tradition is often vague but more grandiloquent and more ambitious of what should be done.

Of course, you can talk about brave new worlds without getting very specific. The political version of the prophets gives you something like a lot of Great Society programs. Or so it seems to me.

But people should have a vision of a good life. A political version of the rabbinic tradition gives you a much more decent society where people understand where their obligations are, rich and poor alike, and where the question of individual rights is secondary. It doesn't sound compassionate, but in fact it's very much concerned with the poor, very much concerned with the sick. It keeps putting things in terms of your obligations to them. Not your rights. But the obligations can be the obverse of many of what we call rights.

I know I have a vision for society, what will make a decent

life. But how we will live together depends on so many other circumstances beyond my control or anyone else's control that I
don't know if you can really talk about a vision of a good society.
We've had lots of visions of a good society—a whole library full
of visions of a good society. Pick and choose, it doesn't really matter. But a vision of a good life. That's another matter.

## Nathan Glazer

You want everyone to lead a decent life. You want government not
to interfere with it, if at all possible, but we do have a badly unrav-
eled fabric affecting good parts of society, and we have to try to
put it back together. That would make a better society. But there
I'm at a loss. We don't know how to do it.

I've gotten into the nitty-gritty of issues like public housing or
welfare. I'm concerned with how one manages to implement
these programs, how many things can go wrong, and therefore I'm
more impressed by modest success.

I am not against government keeping on trying and getting
instruction from its own failures and efforts, I'm for that. I believe
in attention to the fine structure, the details, and that perhaps
comes out of my interest in architecture and planning. I don't
think you can give up governmental efforts in any of these areas,
like crime and reconstruction of poor neighborhoods and so on.
But just what those efforts should be, we're still struggling to find
out.

## Daniel Bell

Optimism is a philosophy, pessimism is a character trait. It's hard to
talk about visions. If you have a creed, if you have a belief system,
the vision flows out of that. I don't have a particular belief system.
To the extent that my optimism overcomes my pessimism, I would
say it's a recurrent belief in the idea of utopia. What is against
utopia? Against utopia is arcadia. The dream of a golden past.

The history of the Jews has never really been a golden past, the history of the intellectuals has never really been a golden past. So arcadia may be a false hope, it's a nostalgia. Utopia's always an openness, a possibility. I believe in utopia as a kind of aim, a vision, while also mindful of the risks. Utopia represents ideals, and how can you live without some sense of ideals? It's a necessary way of living. I remain, still, purely a utopian.

*In May 1993, after several years of illness, Irving Howe, still a confirmed socialist, died of heart failure. His final book, a collection of literary essays titled* A Critic's Notebook, *was brought out posthumously by his son Nicholas Howe.*

*After neoconservatism had been declared all but indistinguishable from conservatism by friends and foes alike, there have been tentative rumblings of its reinvigoration. Irving Kristol and others have found themselves increasingly disenchanted with the conservative movement for abandoning the more inclusive, broad-based conservatism of the Reagan years. In 1995, he published a new collection of essays,* Neoconservatism: The Autobiography of an Idea.

*In 1997, Nathan Glazer published a critical but supportive exploration of multiculturalism entitled* We Are All Multiculturalists Now. *Once again, as in his revised stand on affirmative action, Glazer's nuanced approach proved to infuriate those on both the left and right.*

*Daniel Bell has, in recent years, published new editions of several of his books, including* The Cultural Contradictions of Capitalism *and* The Coming of Post-Industrial Society *in addition to founding a new journal,* Correspondence, *that explores international intellectual developments. All three men, now in their late seventies and eighties, have, at least partially, retired and, having failed miserably at this task, seem busier and more argumentative than ever.*

# 10. Worrying with a Purpose

IRVING [HOWE] TAUGHT US TO ARGUE AND TO WORRY. MOST OF US,
I SUPPOSE, NEVER WORRIED ENOUGH, BECAUSE WE ALWAYS KNEW
THAT HE WAS WORRIED, WORRYING STEADILY, WORRYING WITH A
PURPOSE, FOR HE WAS ALSO STUBBORNLY AND STRANGELY, AND
SOMETIMES LUMINOUSLY, HOPEFUL.

—*Michael Walzer*

As a group the New York intellectuals have long since ceased to exist, pulled apart by politics, by cultural change, and, of course, by death. In his 1987 book, *The Last Intellectuals*, Russell Jacoby claimed that the group represented our culture's final generation of public intellectuals, men and women who sought an impact beyond the walls of the university and whose wide-ranging essays were written for a general, if sophisticated, audience. Jacoby's praise for the New York intellectuals was in part an attack on the generation of critics who followed them, men and women who retreated into the academy and lost themselves in the wilds of postmodernist theory; spun off from the flailing juggernaut that the New Left became in its final days, they turned to deconstructing the world, once they had failed to revolutionize it.

In contrast, the New York intellectuals were the products of an era when answers to all questions seemed knowable. When Nathan Glazer explains that "there's . . . an initial arrogance that if you're a Marxist you can understand anything . . . a model that, even as we gave up our Marxism, we nevertheless stuck with," he is describing both an intellectual habit and an ethos. That young theoretical arrogance fueled in each of these men and women a propulsive force of belief, a faith that the world could be made right, if only! That belief is no longer easy to come by.

The understanding that Marxism was not the grand, all-encompassing theory it claimed to be, coupled with the stark realization that the utopian desire to remake the world had led to human catastrophe, left in its wake a more pragmatic, if no less ardent, intellectual impulse. But even in their deradicalization, the members of the New York group did not turn inward. In coming to understand what Lionel Trilling called the "variousness and complexity" of life, the sheer elusiveness of a single overriding truth that could be captured whole by any single theory, they did not lose their passion for intellectual engagement, their hope of acting on the world through the force of their intellect.

As a group, the New York intellectuals were held together by a common love, Modernism, and a common foe, Communism, but they were created in large part by social circumstances. As children of Jewish immigrants, they were caught between the world of their largely uneducated, working-class parents, to which they could not return, and a largely Protestant academia that was not yet open to them as Jews. It was a time when the larger culture was not yet interested in serious ideas. They had no choice but to create their own world.

In time, the university, less parochial after the Second World War and short on faculty, accepted and welcomed them; popular magazines, once indifferent to the New York intellectuals' talents and their ideas (and anathema to the New York group for their lack of seriousness), found themselves in need of new writers for a more sophisticated reading public.

This victory was paired with the triumph of anti-Communism as America's reigning Cold War ideology and the belated academic recognition of the great Modernist writers. With nothing in common left to fight for and no one left to fight against, the inevitable result was the gradual dissolution of the New Yorkers as a cohesive group. But if anything, their individual careers flourished as the group itself withered, and they never stopped fighting, never stopped arguing, never stopped "worrying with a purpose," in Michael Walzer's phrase.

In a way that must have seemed both thrilling and disorienting, the group triumphantly arrived on the cultural scene just at the moment when America had begun to achieve a kind of cultural dominance, at least in the Western world. The New York intellectuals had long looked to Europe for their cultural role models, and while they remained strongly aware of their indebtedness to their European counterparts, they could not help but be aware of their new place in the world with the burgeoning of American art and literature.

They welcomed all this success, their acceptance by the larger American culture, and their new footing in Europe, but they did so with a certain anxiety. Who else but the New York intellectuals would have openly wrung their hands at the thought of their own triumph, as they did in the *Partisan Review* symposium, "Our Country and Our Culture," published in two consecutive issues of the journal in 1952. The editors explained that:

> The purpose of this symposium is to examine the apparent fact that American intellectuals now regard America and its institutions in a new way. Until little more than a decade ago, America was commonly thought to be hostile to art and culture. Since then, however, the tide has begun to turn, and many writers and intellectuals now feel closer to their country and its culture. . . . We have obviously come a long way from the earlier rejection of America as spiritually barren . . . and the Marxist picture of America in the thirties as a land of capitalist reaction. . . . For better or worse, most writers no longer accept alienation as the artist's fate in America; on the contrary, they want very much to be a part of American life.
>
> [But] do you believe that a democratic society necessari-

ly leads to a levelling of culture, to a mass culture which will overrun intellectual and aesthetic values traditional to Western Civilization?

[And] if a reaffirmation and rediscovery of America is under way, can the tradition of critical non-conformism (going back to Thoreau and Melville and embracing some of the major expressions of American intellectual history) be maintained as strongly as ever?

In this symposium the editors and contributors to *Partisan Review* were attempting to grapple with the potential loss of intellectual standards in a democratic, capitalist culture that works to homogenize and popularize serious thought even as it embraces the thinker. They were also clearly worrying over the intellectual's loss of critical function in a society he has come more to accept— if critically—than to reject. This last was a particularly acute issue for a group of Jewish former Marxists who once felt themselves twice-alienated, first from capitalism and then from America's Protestant-dominated culture.

But behind the intellectual questions one also senses the anxiety of a group who, despite having striven for and even courted success, find themselves suddenly put off balance by having achieved the readership and influence they had sought for so long. The New York intellectuals could not simply accept this state of affairs at face value; they had to examine it and argue about it. In this symposium, there were decidedly mixed reactions to the state of American culture. While amply acknowledging American weaknesses, Lionel Trilling nevertheless remained convinced of a cultural transformation:

For the first time in the history of the modern American intellectual, America is not to be conceived of as *a priori* the vulgarest and stupidest nation in the world. And this is not only because other nations are exercising as never before the inalienable right of nations to be stupid and vulgar. The American situation has changed in a way that is not merely relative. There is an unmistakable improvement in the present American cultural situation over that of, say, thirty years ago.

Among others, Irving Howe spoke out strongly against what he perceived as his friends' slow tumble toward the abyss of political and, to a lesser degree, cultural contentment. Two years later, Howe would use the pages of that same magazine, *Partisan Review*, with the acquiescence of its editors, to attack his fellow intellectuals for their conformity, occasioning more bitter arguments. Howe, who had stayed to the political left of his friends, was criticizing their politics—their support for the Cold War, among other things—but clearly it was the very notion of marginality as an intellectual calling card, as an essential part of one's *bona fides*, that was at stake as the group was accepted and ultimately lauded by a wider American society.

Understanding the importance of marginality to the group is a key to understanding the mind-set of the New York intellectuals and the somewhat odd puzzle of their ambivalence over success. The question remained, for them, how could they safeguard their intellectual integrity, their intellectual independence, in the midst of their success? After all, it was just this, the loss of independence, as Neil Jumonville points out in his study of the group, *Critical Crossings*, that lay behind their attack on those intellectuals subservient to the political program of Communism. Politically, the New Yorkers always maintained a stubborn independence.

Howe maintained his vital sense of marginality in his political life even as he became a distinguished literary critic and professor of literature. A socialist to the end, he had no fear that his political voice would find any ready acceptance in a country whose very identity is steeped in the capitalist ethos. But neither would Bell, Glazer, or even Kristol fully relinquish their sense of themselves as critics and outsiders, despite Howe's criticisms. Bell became a liberal, but never a wholly contented one, at times criticizing the Democratic party from the right for its soft-headed, romantic views of social change in the sixties, and later from the left, for its lack of dedication to providing economically for the dispossessed. Bell, a man wary of labels, continues to call himself a conservative in culture, a liberal in politics, and a socialist in economics. How can a man like this ever be counted fully at home in any one place? He is a man who thrives, as the others do, on cutting against the grain.

If Bell disdains the crudeness and "one-dimensionality" of labels, it would seem that Nathan Glazer barely knows or cares that they exist. Glazer, like Bell, actively resists the categorization of his thought, instinctively confounding his would-be allies on the right and left with his perpetually evolving conceptions of social issues. Glazer's pragmatism in matters of public policy may have been frustrating to conservatives and liberals alike, but it has allowed him to work with Irving Kristol for years while voting Democratic and maintaining strong ties to the liberal community. Having written an attack on affirmative action in the seventies, he has become a latter-day defender of it because of his belief in the need to maintain the presence of African Americans in colleges and universities. In his youth, Glazer managed to be a Marxist and binational Zionist, even though Marxism stresses internationalism and Zionism is predicated on the importance of Israel as an explicitly Jewish state; at middle age, he was a self-described mild conservative with radical tendencies; in later years, he has been a liberal defender of Ronald Reagan's social policies. It is not so much that Glazer is a man of contradictions, but that he is almost wholly free of the need for the comfort of labels, of the desire to be part of any kind of permanent political alliance. He is a happy party of one.

Unlike their friends, Irving Howe and Irving Kristol have embraced political movements, but more out of the perceived need for a theoretical basis for their political action than any attraction to the simplifying verities that ideological conviction demands. Howe, as his colleague Michael Walzer remembered, clung to socialism because he did not want the dream of social equality embodied by socialism to die. "Irving's view has been that one doesn't want to be the end of that line. One doesn't want to give up on that project," Walzer explained.

And yet Howe, unable to dismiss complex truths, had discarded many of his early socialist convictions by the end of his life and knew that his socialist beliefs "sound[ed] vague." There was a sense of frustrated concession in Howe, as there was an equal frustration on the part of many of Howe's political opponents, that he refused to stop calling himself a socialist long after he had given up many of socialism's central tenets. And yet what Howe reveals is his own refusal to narrow his thought into a single ideological channel when faced with the messy realities of the world around him. For those, like Daniel Bell, who remembered Howe's youthful ideological rigidity at City College, the great change that he had undergone over the course of his life was all the more remarkable.

Irving Kristol, poles apart from Howe politically and temperamentally, was virtually the only so-called neoconservative to accept the label. He believes in the need for a political agenda and is part of a political movement, as Howe was until his death. The most purely political of the four—he lives in Washington, D.C., and has played a major behind-the-scenes role in the Republican party—Kristol still maintains a careful personal distance from politics and government. He cannot bear to be wholly a party man. The same sixteen-year-old who preferred to remain on the periphery of the Trotskyists has become a force in Republican politics by remaining in his perch as coeditor of *The Public Interest*, free to criticize and instruct.

A power broker who helped many others gain positions in the Reagan administration, Kristol himself is unwilling to fully relinquish his place as an outsider. Since I first began talking with him more than ten years ago, he has moved from neoconservatism to conservatism and back again, ultimately realizing that he had lived his life on the margins of many movements. "Ever since I can remember," Kristol recalled, "I've been a neo-something, a neo-Marxist, a neo-Trotskyist, a neo-liberal, a neo-conservative, and in religion always a neo-Orthodox, even while I was a neo-Trotskyist and a neo-Marxist. I'm going to end up a neo. Just neo, that's all. Neo-dash-nothing."

And yet, these writers who cut their intellectual teeth on the very idea of marginality, on a belief in the virtue of critical distance from one's culture, clearly desired influence. Ironically, but understandably, it was their early outsider status that prompted their interest in political and cultural movements that emphasized the universal: Marxism and Modernism were movements that, at least theoretically, saw in the conditions of modernity both the possibility and the necessity for remaking the world. Even in their youthful radical vision of the world, the very idea of America played an important role. In Todd Gitlin's words, they felt "that the New World afforded the possibility for the living out of the great universalist vision that had its nurturance in Europe and that was rooted intellectually in Marxism and morally in socialist values."

If, in their emphasis on the universal, they did not entirely suppress their Jewish identity, it took them a number of years to find a place for it in their intellectual lives. Moreover, even as they came to embrace their Jewishness after the war, they never ceased being universalists above all. They did not then and do not now think of themselves as Jewish intellectuals, but as intellectuals who happen to be Jewish. When they did plumb their own Jewish identity it was with the assumption that their search would yield answers with universal implications.

The sea-change wrought by the sixties and the identity politics it spawned inspired a generation to reject the universalism so prized by the New York group. Following a path initially laid out by Irving Howe in his reclamation of his Yiddish heritage, many younger writers and critics—Jewish, African American, and feminist—have chosen to embrace their distinctive identities and to understand the world primarily through their particularity. At its worst, multiculturalism became a license for separatism and an attack on the very idea of an intellectual community and of meaningful intellectual dialogue. But the desire to be rooted in one's ethnic past is also the natural preoccupation of later generations who have felt themselves from the beginning to be more securely a part of American culture while at the same time desirous of a connection to their ethnic past. The literary critic Morris Dickstein first encountered New York intellectuals like Lionel Trilling as an undergraduate at Columbia University in the late fifties and went on to become a contributing editor to *Partisan Review*. "By and large," he recalls, "when I came on the scene in the early sixties, one of the main bones I had to pick with my elders was the degree of embarrassment they obviously had with where they came from and their Jewish identity. In the sixties this notion of authenticity came to the fore. Not only 'Do your own thing,' but 'Be your own self.' I think the need of earlier generations to pass and to gain acceptance in America as Americans was replaced by our need to show our colors."

The cultural expansion, which conspired to pull apart the New York intellectuals, has been equally responsible for preventing the rise of another group quite like it. The very diversity of intellectual culture and the rise of the academy in American life over the past fifty years has meant the dissolution of a unitary intellectual culture (if in fact this was ever the case) and the retreat by many into a world of academic theorizing incomprehensible to the public. Russell Jacoby explained that the New York group "represented a kind of intellectual life, which is increasingly difficult, which is rare. Some people can buck the trend, some people can resist, and certainly many people have. But it's difficult. They represented a kind of intellectual life and commitment, which is endangered, which is hard to revitalize.

The infrastructure is disappearing, the small independent journals, the cheap apartments, the benign city life, which allowed this intellectual life to continue. The university has encouraged a very different kind of intellectual style."

That university-based intellectual style is dominated by specialization rather than generalization, by the need to speak to one's academic peers rather than the larger public, and by the insistence on credentialed knowledge as opposed to the intellectual forays of the inspired amateur. In these ways the university can encourage a professionalized narrowness of interests at the expense of placing one's work in a larger social and cultural context. Bell, Kristol, Glazer, and Howe were part of a transitional generation whose roots lay in the old prewar intellectual culture bred in the city's streets, diners, and coffeehouses (not to mention the City College cafeteria), but whose education was refined and enlarged by the university in the postwar years. None of these men got a traditional graduate school education (though Glazer and Bell did do graduate work and were ultimately awarded Ph.D.'s based on published books), but they ultimately sought and found a home in the university—with the exception of Irving Kristol, who nevertheless taught part-time for many years.

Unfortunately, the inevitable need to specialize was abetted by the rise of "theory"—imported from Europe—which was seized on by Jacoby's disillusioned sixties radicals, those who had moved into university English and history departments and had become known as the academic left. For the most part, this theory itself became a wall that divorced its adherents from the world. It encouraged detachment rather than engagement, arguing that "truth" was not merely elusive but unattainable and that "reality" was quicksand that left no room for constructive engagement, no means of acting on the world. The process of self-immurement was secured by a thicket of jargon and abstruse concepts that rendered the writings of the adherents of theory impenetrable to the lay reader. Paul Berman, an essayist and former New Leftist who resisted the academy, comments, "The academic left was missing any kind of literary sensibility and the other thing that was missing was something as simple as common sense. There was nothing to prevent them from going over every cliff in sight. Beginning first with the realization that those people couldn't write well, you could arrive at the further realization that not only couldn't they write, they couldn't think."

As Berman points out, one of those things that defined the New York intellectuals was their appreciation of and ability to write the well-crafted essay. "A New York intellectual is writer or editor or anyone at all who likes to read and think about a certain kind of essay, which I would describe this way: An essay about culture or politics or the arts, written in a spirit that is not entirely Olympian or distant—an essay that is ardent for ideas, maybe even for an idea of social progress, and is just as ardent for the arts. And it is an essay written in a fairly specific style, in a voice that is human and not institutional—literate, intelligent, conversational, though also maybe a little urgent—an essay that might have some literary merit in itself. "

But if something has been lost in the rise of the university, something too has been gained. As Glazer knew, "It was specialize or die," not simply because the culture demanded it, but because the "large pronouncement" must ultimately have some kind of basis in a discipline of knowledge, even if the largest pronouncements ultimately are grounded in one's experience, in knowledge that is the fruit of one's personal history as well. Writing in the online magazine *Slate* in 1999, Bell defended his long-standing interest in theory as a guide to knowledge, while wryly recounting the story "of the young man drafted into the Israeli navy who, when asked if he knew how to swim, replied, 'I know the theory of it.'" At the same time, experiential knowledge alone is limiting. To swim in the deepest intellectual waters, one must have access to both theory and experience and this the four men had by virtue of their upbringing and later education.

The expansion of university culture has, in fact, provided many would-be intellectuals with the livelihood and institutional base necessary to engage in their best work, and in this sense it has provided an expansion of intellectual culture in this country as never before. But in decentralizing intellectual culture, universities have also helped to fragment it. The New York intellectuals, like it or not, were in their heyday—as Norman Podhoretz remarked, "stuck with one another"—in the precincts of the city. But long ago Glazer moved to Berkeley, California, and then, along with Bell, to Cambridge, Massachusetts. In the late eighties Kristol moved to Washington, D.C. Howe, alone among his friends, remained in New York (with the exception of a few short forays elsewhere) until his death in 1993.

The New York intellectuals maintained their independence in large part by the creation and editing of their own journals even as they began to work in mainstream journalistic and academic institutions. They were not so foolish as to ignore the benefits of pay and of prestige that came with this new work. Nor were they so blind as not to understand the importance of maintaining a niche for a writing more sophisticated than that allowed in mass-circulation magazines and, at the same time, more accessible than that desired by academic publications. Today, economics has forced most intellectual journals to affiliate with the academy or to seek out a mass audience. That mediating niche remains more elusive than ever.

The culture at large has also necessarily fragmented intellectual life, not simply by offering intellectuals a greater number of outlets and a potentially larger reading public, but by its very diversity. In the absence of the Cold War, political and intellectual life has lost an overriding organizing principle, as surely as has American foreign policy. The new multipolar world is a fact of intellectual life as it is of diplomacy and trade. The New York intellectuals were oriented toward Europe, from which their families had fled and which was the birthplace and graveyard of the revolutionary socialist ideal. But as the intellectual community has diversified, its sights have been turned to other parts of the globe.

In recent years the New York group has been criticized for its deafness to issues of race. Although they were all supporters of the civil rights movement, and the journals of the New York intellectual community commented extensively about the events of the sixties, none of the individuals were actively involved. For some critics, this became a more egregious fault in light of the strong and vocal neoconservative attack on affirmative action programs in the seventies. But what these criticisms often fail to take into account is that in the New York intellectual world, black writers were accepted in a way that few other groups or institutions could match. Randall Kennedy, a professor of law at Harvard University, explains that though a lack of attention to racial issues "was true of many of the New York intellectuals and was a problem, it's also true that if one goes back through *Commentary*, through *Partisan Review*, through *Dissent* magazine, what does one see? Some of the early essays—and best essays—of James Baldwin, Ralph Ellison, and Richard Wright."

It has remained for more recent generations to alter the intellectual landscape for African Americans in part as a reaction against the New York group and, in part, because of the groundwork laid out by those black intellectuals who formed an extended part of the group.

Some have pointed to the African American intellectuals currently clustered at Harvard University as the nearest successors to the New York intellectuals. Henry Louis Gates, Cornel West, William Julius Wilson, Orlando Patterson, and Kennedy himself, among others, combine intellectual scholarship with strong public voices and wide-ranging interests; the group includes a literary scholar, a philosopher, a law professor, and a sociologist. At the same time, these thinkers are drawn together by their interest in

the role of race in American society, giving them a common subject much as the New York intellectuals were bound together by
their anti-Communism. Race, like anti-Communism, is an issue
where the deep personal passions of these intellectuals intersect
with the critical concerns of the society at large. And like the New
Yorkers, they have used this issue to explore universal values and
to carry their concerns to a larger public. Yet Randall Kennedy
believes that the Harvard group lacks the cohesiveness of their
New York predecessors: "There have been magazines—I attempted one—but none of them have had the broad range, the panache,
the influence of a *Partisan Review*. There's no African American
publication that comes close to a *Partisan Review*, or for that matter
a *Commentary* or a *Dissent*." The reason lies, perhaps, in the fact
that these African American intellectuals grew up inside the academy, and did not come late to it, as did the New York intellectuals.
They have never had quite the same need for an independent
intellectual platform. "At an earlier time," Kennedy points out,
"there were the *Journal of Negro History* and *Journal of Negro Education*, which were created out of necessity because the *American
Historical Review* was closed to blacks, for the most part. But nowadays, with the white organs of opinion being open to blacks and
being very welcoming, for the most part, there is no counterpart
to *Partisan Review*."

A number of intellectual magazines still thrive today, in and
out of the academy, but none bring together a group in quite the
way that *Partisan Review* once did, not *Partisan Review* itself, not
even its intellectual offspring, like *Commentary*, *Dissent*, *The Public
Interest*, *The New York Review of Books*, or the book review section
of *The New Republic*. The very proliferation of mass-market magazines willing to publish—and pay—"serious" writers prevents any
ambitious but small journal from attracting, holding on to, and
ultimately defining a group of writers in the way that *PR* could in
its postwar heyday.

In the end, the question of successor groups to the New York intellectuals is less important than the fact that a number of individuals have carried on their work: the attempt at cultural and political criticism that is wide-ranging in its interests, well-written, and meant for a serious, nonacademic audience. Over the years, many in the New York group have reached out to younger intellectuals. Randall Kennedy can remember contacting Alfred Kazin as he was writing an undergraduate dissertation on Kazin's old friend, Richard Hofstadter. "He took me out to the Century Club," Kennedy recalls. "Here I was, only nineteen or twenty, and we talked for hours. Irving Howe was another person I got to know through this senior thesis. I got the sense from Kazin, I got the sense from Howe, that these were people who took me seriously."

Mark Lilla, a political scientist at the University of Chicago's Committee on Social Thought, found his way to *The Public Interest* after taking a course with Bell at Harvard. He worked at the magazine in the early eighties under Irving Kristol and has, in recent years, worked closely with Bell on a new international journal of arts and politics called *Correspondence*. Of his time at *The Public Interest*, Lilla recalls that "we would have lunch in the office every day. At about twelve o'clock while we were working, Irving would suddenly shout out, a propos of nothing, 'I'll have a cheeseburger.' We would then take an order for everyone else. To encourage us to write, Irving paid us absolutely nothing (about eleven thousand dollars), instead he fed us. We could order whatever we wanted, and that was our big meal of the day. But it was also our time to be with him, time I would use to ask him questions about books. I would ask him what he thought about Freud on Moses, about Hegel on history, or what I had been reading in Leo Strauss, and we would just talk over lunch. It was a running seminar where I began getting my first real education." Paul Berman found his model in Irving Howe, and Morris Dickstein grew close to Alfred Kazin over the years.

Though a younger generation of women found their way to

the group, they did not find the same kind of relationships, but then women never had in this group. If the New York intellectuals did provide a kind of rough democracy of intellect that recognized talent regardless of sex, women remained, in most ways, socially inferior. In this world many bright women took second place intellectually to their husbands and, as Diana Trilling pointed out, often needed a stiff drink or two just to make it through some of the group's parties. At the same time, what other contemporary circle could claim so many strong female voices, among them Gertrude Himmelfarb, the distinguished historian who is also the wife of Irving Kristol, the novelists Mary McCarthy and Elizabeth Hardwick, and the political philosopher, Hannah Arendt. Trilling herself did her best work in the years after the death of her husband in 1975.

Those women, like Trilling, who did write were, at times, accorded hypocritical treatment, chairing a meeting one moment, cleaning up after it the next. Barbara Probst Solomon, a novelist and essayist who came to know the group in the late fifties, remembers her difficulty, as a woman, in being taken seriously. "Most of the women in that group were pretty fearful and therefore not easily approachable," she recalls. "There were few women my age and probably not unattached ones. I stayed away from most of the older women because they terrified me more than the men did. One of them once came up to me and asked, 'Are you the secretary at *Commentary*?'

Daphne Merkin, who writes for *The New Yorker*, feels that "the differing nature of a certain kind of female intellectual style accounts, in part, for the lack of a stronger connection." The New York group, despite their interest in the arts and their connection to novelists like McCarthy and Saul Bellow, were a group more comfortable with critical reasoning as opposed to a more purely aesthetic experience that grows out of the personal and specifically the emotional. Women "who were drenched in sensibility, both as people and in that their intellects were pervaded by it," had, according to Merkin, "more trouble" being recognized.

The very difficulty in defining the nature of the intellectual is part of the problem of defining just who is one. The historian or economist or literature professor can point to established credentials, but the idea of credentials, in the purely academic sense, is antithetical to the idea of an unmediated relationship to the life of the mind. Even trickier is attempting to adduce examples of the influence an intellectual or group of intellectuals have on the life of their culture. But nevertheless there is work one can point to, ideas nurtured, and younger generations, such as those mentioned, who have taken inspiration from the group.

Kristol never really joined the academy, despite his stints of teaching, but even Glazer, Bell, and Howe, who spent the better part of their lives as professors, were never quite *of* the academy. In much the same way that their political thought is uncategorizable by conventional labels, so their intellectual careers have wandered through many streams, their interests spilling over from one to another. Glazer is often described as a sociologist, yet his appointment at Harvard was in the graduate school of education, and his many books have explored the Communist party, American Judaism, ethnicity, and urban affairs. Though Bell's work over the last several decades has focused on a theory of contemporary society, his earlier work has spanned education, socialism, the labor movement, and religion. In addition to his literary work, Howe was a leading socialist intellectual, a Yiddishist, and a historian of Jewish culture. Kristol is known primarily as a political intellectual, and yet his own interests range broadly to philosophy and religion. And all have remained tied to the world of highbrow journalism, Kristol and Glazer through *The Public Interest*; Howe until his death through *Dissent*; while Bell, now eighty years old, has spent his retirement creating—along with colleagues from Japan and Germany—the new quarterly journal *Correspondence*, which reports on new artistic and political developments around the world.

The group, as Irving Howe wrote in *The New York Intellectuals*, came late to Modernism. Many of the great works of modern literature had already been written by the time *Partisan Review* was first published, but there is no question that the group played a critical part in introducing Modernism into the university and into mainstream culture as professors and literary critics. And the art critics Clement Greenberg, Harold Rosenberg, and Meyer Schapiro played key roles in championing the works of the then-unknown Abstract Expressionist painters in the late forties and early fifties.

As for the group's other central preoccupation, anti-Communism, there can be little doubt that, in the long run, their ideas proved victorious. Though at times overzealous in their attacks on Communists as unfit to teach and, in their fury over the duplicity of the party itself, blind to the effects of McCarthyism on individual lives, their analysis of Communism at home and abroad proved on the whole strikingly accurate. Their insistence that the American Communist party was controlled and funded by Moscow and was engaged in espionage has been corroborated by the opening of Soviet government archives. The guilt of Julius Rosenberg (and the innocence of his wife, Ethel) along with that of accused spy Alger Hiss are accepted by all but a few diehard supporters. It is true that they did not predict the fall of the Soviet Union, but then its sudden demise surprised most everyone.

Part of their legacy resides in the example of their public careers, which have inspired men and women to bridge the worlds of serious scholarship and public life. Even in the forties and fifties, as Irving Kristol recalls, "The gap between academics and intellectuals was a real one. If you were writing a review of a book by someone, and wanted to be nasty, you would say he had written an 'academic' book. On the other hand, if an academic were writing a review of a book by an intellectual in a more academic journal and he wanted to be nasty, he would say his book is 'brilliant,' meaning unsound!" But with the rise of theory in the academy, the chasm became deeper. "As a reaction against academic specialization and jargon in the seventies and eighties, the notion of the public intellectual emerged," explains Morris Dickstein. "People began to look back at the New York intellectuals as the last serious group of intellectuals who had been both academically qualified and yet played a significant public role."

But in recent years, the popularity of the idea has led some to react against the term. Randall Kennedy worries that the very idea of the "public intellectual" as opposed to the "academic scholar" has become an excuse. "I do get the nagging suspicion that the 'public intellectual' niche can become a refuge from rigor," Kennedy explains. Mark Lilla concurs: "I'm not alone in finding the term 'public intellectual' to be a problem. Those who have appropriated it are not people I can associate myself with. Most of them are politicized academics whose highest ambition is to appear on the op-ed page of the *The New York Times*." In these fears one hears an echo of the worry expressed in the 1952 "Our Country and Our Culture" symposium that the popularization of intellectual life will come at the expense of truly serious thought.

Mark Lilla believes that "this unmediated relation to the life of the mind and the life of the spirit, this directness in relation to literature or to philosophy or to music, is disappearing. The reasons for this change are deep and have to do with larger changes in society. People read less today, so they write less well, and nobody has the time or interest for reflection. Younger people today have been shaped by a system of mass higher education, not the little world of magazines and books. The university has expanded, and corporate journalism has become omnipresent, absorbing all these people who in an earlier age might have aimed a little higher. The university especially stifles the kind of immediacy I'm talking about; people who become professors today don't even know what it means. They are cultural spectators looking at the life of the spirit with binoculars, placing everything in its proper historical context. The younger intellectuals I admire are those who have a soft spot in their hearts for the world of the little magazine, who love good writing and feel themselves at home with those who actually create important works of the spirit."

Given that we live in a world dominated by television and film, in a culture in which communication is expressed primarily in images and the spoken word, it is perhaps unsurprising that the world centered on writing has suffered, and with it an intellectual culture that demands the written word for expression and that depends on a reading public for its transmission. But the question remains, how large has this culture ever been? Daphne Merkin quotes Jules Renard: "All paradises are lost paradises." According to Morris Dickstein, "What people tend to forget is how little public audience they had during their heyday, that a lot of the shine on them has been retrospective. People tend to think that in the forties everybody waited with bated breath for the next word of Trilling or Philip Rahv or so on but at the time they tended to speak to a relatively small group but in a distinctly public and accessible style. Their careers have been rewritten to make them like figures who might address a public within a quite different media age."

The cultural transformation that began in the fifties and that brought about mass culture and the rise of mass higher education—the very changes to which the "Our Country and Our Culture" symposium was a reaction—has so altered the landscape of intellectual life that it becomes difficult to gain the proper perspective. The change in context, the alteration in the cultural backdrop against which intellectual life takes place, plays havoc with our ability to see it in comparison to what has gone before, to the world in which the New York intellectuals first found their voice.

"The New York intellectuals," according to Dickstein, "thrived in a period where there was a very sharp separation between a kind of middlebrow or mass culture scene that was relatively philistine by the standards of the Modernists and a rather elite group of self-constituted intellectuals who were really comfortable talking primarily to each other. Those extremes have dissolved and a large amorphous middle has been created in which a lot of what was formerly intellectual discourse has infiltrated into glossy magazines like *Vanity Fair* or *The New Yorker* and a lot of what was formerly popular culture has become an important part of the intellectual discourse, questions about television, the popular culture, movies, and so on. The map of the cultural scene has changed. The missing middle, the gap between high culture or the avant-garde and mass culture has now given way to a larger ground in between in which people have been attracted to comment on public issues and also, in the process, become some form of media celebrity on their own."

There are, in other words, many more writers and critics than there have ever been, though they do not necessarily engage the issues of politics and culture with the high seriousness that was the trademark of the New York intellectuals. Though there is much cultural battling, particularly between left and right, these fights do not, in most cases, add up to the "life of significant contention" that, in Diana Trilling's memorable words, marked the struggles of the New York group. But perhaps it is also true that even as the numbers of serious intellectuals has increased, they must now attempt to reach one another across a wider and less easily delineated cultural landscape, one whose interests are more scattered. Today the culture of media celebrity acts to distract the public from serious thought and parades glibness and facility of speech as profundity. Even years after television has become a staple of our lives, Bell, Glazer, and Kristol make only rare appearances in a medium they neither feel entirely comfortable with nor trust to transmit their ideas.

"Did they capture the public imagination until recently," wondered Daphne Merkin, "or simply each other's imagination and it had enough of an 'echo,' as Diana Trilling put it?" The New York intellectuals, walled off from the popular culture, were oddly confident that their thoughts would resonate within the larger culture. "The notion that someone is listening in on the argument is almost nonexistent today," Merkin continued. "The sense that what one felt about the ideas of the day was of interest to the world at large has faded. I'm unclear that the world ever listened as much as we think it did. I think interest in them was always fairly small; I think it is much smaller now." Perhaps expectations are different in an age of mass culture when popular film and television can regularly command audiences in the millions. Writing amidst this distracting—though largely vacuous—plenty, the intellectual can only feel lonelier, his or her echo less resonant.

Still, what was habit to a generation that made its way into the academy through the world of the intellectual journal has become a model to those who have been intellectually raised in academe but understand the advantage of "thinking out loud" beyond its boundaries. These men and women remain, like the New York intellectuals, interested in continuing a conversation that takes into account the relationship of politics and culture, and they cannot help but ask the serious questions. In Michael Walzer's description of the New York group, they are writers who feel that "you can't begin to analyze the most recent strike in Detroit without starting from the division of labor in ancient Babylonia. The context is world history and the questions you bring to your analysis are the largest questions: Where are we going? Where have we been?"

The New York intellectuals continue to loom large in the imaginations of many younger intellectuals today, in part because of the work they have done that endures, and in part because their lives represent the possibility of enduring and passionate intellectual engagement. The contours of intellectual life continue to change, but in looking backward to this group, as so many have done, one gains not only a respect for past accomplishment but also a sense that in the example of their lives lies a key to the future of serious thought.

# Selected Bibliography

Much of this book is based on a series of interviews I videotaped for the documentary film, which are now being held in the oral history archives of Columbia University in New York City. The following is a list of additional resources drawn on in the making of the film and book.

Aaron, Daniel. *Writers on the Left*. New York: Harcourt, Brace and World, 1961.

Abel, Lionel. *The Intellectual Follies: A Memoir of the Literary Venture in New York and Paris*. New York: Norton, 1984.

Barrett, William. *The Truants: Adventures Among the Intellectuals*. New York: Anchor Press, 1983.

Bell, Daniel. *The Coming of Post-Industrial Society*. New York: Basic Books, 1973. (Reissued 1999.)

——. *The Cultural Contradictions of Capitalism*. New York: Basic Books, 1976.

——. *The End of Ideology: On the Exhaustion of Political Ideas in the Fifties*. Glencoe, Ill.: The Free Press, 1960. (Reissued by Harvard University Press, 1988.)

——. *Marxian Socialism in the United States*. Princeton, N.J.: Princeton University Press, 1967. (Reissued by Cornell University Press, 1996.)

——. *Reforming of General Education: The Columbia College Experience in Its National Setting*. New York: Columbia University Press, 1966. (Reissued by Transaction Press, 2000.)

——. *The Winding Passage: Essays and Sociological Journeys 1960–1980*. Cambridge: Abt Books, 1980.

Bell, Daniel, and Irving Kristol, eds. *Confrontation: The Student Rebellion and the Universities*. New York: Basic Books, 1969.

Bellow, Saul. *The Adventures of Augie March*. New York: Viking Press, 1953.

Bender, Thomas. *New York Intellect: A History of Intellectual Life in New York from 1750 to the Beginnings of Our Own Time*. New York: Alfred Knopf, 1987.

Bloom, Alexander. *Prodigal Sons: The New York Intellectuals and Their World*. New York: Oxford University Press, 1986.

Blumenthal, Sidney. *The Rise of the Counter-Establishment: From Conservative Ideology to Political Power*. New York: Harper and Row, 1986.

Brick, Howard. *Daniel Bell and the Decline of Intellectual Radicalism: Social Theory and Political Reconciliation in the 1940s*. Madison: University of Wisconsin Press, 1986.

Caute, David. *The Fellow Travellers: Intellectual Friends of Communism*. New Haven: Yale University Press, 1988.

Coleman, Peter. *The Liberal Conspiracy: The Congress for Cultural Freedom and the Struggle for the Mind of Postwar Europe*. New York: Free Press, 1989.

Cooney, Terry. *The Rise of the New York Intellectuals:* Partisan Review *and Its Circles 1934–1945*. New York: Harper and Row, 1985.

Dash Moore, Deborah. *At Home in America: Second Generation New York Jews*. New York: Columbia University Press, 1981.

Dickstein, Morris. *Gates of Eden: American Culture in the Sixties*. New York: Penguin Books, 1989.

Diggins, John Patrick. *The Proud Decades: America in War and Peace, 1941–1960*. New York: Norton, 1988.

Draper, Theodore. *American Communism and Soviet Russia*. New York: Vintage Books, 1986.

Fox, Richard. *Reinhold Niebuhr: A Biography*. New York: Harper and Row, 1985.

Fried, Richard M. *Nightmare in Red: The McCarthy Era in Perspective*. New York: Oxford University Press, 1990.

Gitlin, Todd. *The Sixties: Years of Hope, Days of Rage*. New York: Bantam, 1987.

Glazer, Nathan. *Affirmative Discrimination: Ethnic Inequality and Public Policy*. New York: Basic Books, 1975. (Reissued by Harvard University Press, 1989.)

——. *American Judaism*. Chicago: University of Chicago Press, 1957. (Reissued 1989.)

——. *Remembering the Answers: Essays on the American Student Revolt*. New York: Basic Books, 1970.

——. *The Social Basis of American Communism*. New York: Harcourt, Brace, 1961.

——. *We Are All Multiculturalists Now*. Cambridge: Harvard University Press, 1997.

Glazer, Nathan, and Daniel Patrick Moynihan. *Beyond the Melting Pot: The Negroes, Puerto Ricans, Jews, Italians, and Irish of New York City*. Cambridge: MIT Press, 1963.

Gorelick, Sherry. *City College and the Jewish Poor 1900–1920*. New Brunswick: Rutgers University Press, 1985.

Hellman, Lillian. *Scoundrel Time*. New York: Little Brown, 1976.

Hertzberg, Arthur. *The Jews in America: Four Centuries of an Uneasy Encounter.* New York: Simon and Schuster, 1989.

Hofstadter, Richard. *Anti-Intellectualism in American Life.* New York: Alfred Knopf, 1962.

Hook, Sidney. *Out of Step: An Unquiet Life in the 20th Century.* New York: Carroll and Graf, 1987.

Howe, Irving. *A Margin of Hope.* New York: Harcourt, Brace and Jovanovich, 1982.

———. *Politics and the Novel.* New York: Horizon Press, 1957. (Reissued by Columbia University Press, 1992.)

———. *Selected Writings 1950–1990.* New York: Harcourt, Brace and Jovanovich, 1992.

———. *Socialism in America.* New York: Harcourt, Brace and Jovanovich, 1985.

———. *World of Our Fathers: The Journey of the East European Jews to America and the Life They Found and Made.* New York: Simon and Schuster, 1976. (Reissued by Schocken Books, 1989.)

Howe, Irving, and Eliezer Greenberg (editors). *A Treasury of Yiddish Stories.* New York: Viking Press, 1954. (Reissued by Penguin Books, 1990.)

Isserman, Maurice. *If I Had a Hammer: The Death of the Old Left and the Birth of the New.* New York: Basic Books, 1987.

Jacoby, Russell. *The Last Intellectuals: American Culture in the Age of Academe.* New York: Basic Books, 1987.

Jumonville, Neil. *Critical Crossings: The New York Intellectuals in Postwar America.* Berkeley: University of California Press, 1991.

Kazin, Alfred. *Starting Out in the Thirties.* Ithaca: Cornell University Press, 1989.

———. *A Walker in the City.* New York: Harcourt, Brace, 1951.

Klehr, Harvey. *The Heyday of American Communism: The Depression Decade.* New York: Basic Books, 1984.

Klehr, Harvey et al. *The Secret World of American Communism.* New Haven: Yale University Press, 1995.

Kristol, Irving. *Neoconservatism: The Autobiography of an Idea: Selected Essays 1949–95.* New York: Free Press, 1995.

———. *On the Democratic Idea in America.* New York: Harper and Row, 1972.

———. *Reflections of a Neoconservative: Looking Back, Looking Ahead.* New York: Basic Books, 1983.

———. *Two Cheers for Capitalism.* New York: Basic Books, 1978.

Laskin, David. *Partisans: Marriage, Politics and Betrayal Among the New York Intellectuals.* New York: Simon & Schuster, 2000.

McCarthy, Mary. *The Company She Keeps.* New York: Harcourt, Brace, and Jovanovich, 1970.

McElvaine, Robert. *The Great Depression: America 1929–1941.* New York: Times Books, 1984.

Matusow, Allen J. *The Unravelling of America: A History of Liberalism in the 1960s*. New York: Harper and Row, 1984.

Miller, James. *Democracy Is in the Streets: From Port Huron to the Siege of Chicago*. New York: Harper and Row, 1985.

Navasky, Victor. *Naming Names*. New York: Viking Press, 1980.

O'Neill, William L. *A Better World: Stalinism and the American Intellectuals*. New Brunswick: Transaction Press, 1990.

——. *Coming Apart: An Informal History of America in the 1960s*. New York: Times Books, 1971.

Pells, Richard. *The Liberal Mind in a Conservative Age: American Intellectuals in the 1940s and 1950s*. New York: Harper and Row, 1985.

Radosh, Ronald, and Joyce Milton. *The Rosenberg File: A Search for the Truth*. New York: Holt, Rinehart and Winston, 1983.

Rorabaugh, W. J. *Berkeley at War: The 1960s*. New York: Oxford University Press, 1989.

Ross, Andrew. *No Respect: Intellectuals and Popular Culture*. New York: Routledge, 1989.

Schlesinger, Arthur. *The Vital Center: The Politics of Freedom*. Boston: Houghton Mifflin, 1949.

Schrecker, Ellen W. *No Ivory Tower: McCarthyism and the Universities*. New York: Oxford University Press, 1986.

Schwartz, Delmore. *In Dreams Begin Responsibilities*. New York: New Directions, 1978.

Simon, Rita James, ed. *As We Saw the Thirties: Essays on Social and Political Movements of a Decade*. Urbana: University of Illinois, 1967.

Steinfels, Peter. *The Neoconservatives: The Men Who Are Changing America's Politics*. New York: Simon and Schuster, 1979.

Teres, Harvey. *Renewing the Left: Politics, Imagination and the New York Intellectuals*. New York: Oxford University Press, 1996.

Trilling, Lionel. *The Middle of the Journey*. New York: Harcourt, Brace and Jovanovich, 1975.

Ulam, Adam. *Stalin: The Man and His Era*. Boston: Beacon Press, 1973.

Wald, Alan. *The New York Intellectuals: The Rise and Fall of the Anti-Stalinist Left from the 1930s to the 1980s*. Chapel Hill: University of North Carolina, 1987.

Wechsler, James. *The Age of Suspicion*. New York: Random House, 1953.

Weisberger, Bernard A. *Cold War, Cold Peace*. New York: American Heritage Press, 1985.

Yergin, Daniel. *Shattered Peace: The Origins of the Cold War*. New York: Penguin Books, 1990.

# Index

JOSEPH DORMAN is an independent filmmaker who has produced numerous documentaries, primarily for public television. His work has also appeared on The Discovery Channel, CBS, and CNN and has been nominated for two Emmy Awards. He lives in New York City.